I0022128

(Old) Rappahannock County, Virginia

Will Book

1682–1687

Ruth and Sam Sparacio

HERITAGE BOOKS
2018

HERITAGE BOOKS
AN IMPRINT OF HERITAGE BOOKS, INC.

Books, CDs, and more—Worldwide

For our listing of thousands of titles see our website
at
www.HeritageBooks.com

Published 2018 by
HERITAGE BOOKS, INC.
Publishing Division
5810 Ruatan Street
Berwyn Heights, Md. 20740

Copyright © Ruth and Sam Sparacio

All rights reserved. No part of this book may be reproduced or transmitted in any form or by any means, electronic or mechanical, including photocopying, recording or by any information storage and retrieval system without written permission from the author, except for the inclusion of brief quotations in a review.

International Standard Book Number
Paperbound: 978-16-8034-918-4

(OLD) RAPPAHANNAOCK COUNTY, VIRGINIA
Wills, Settlements of Estates, Transcript of Book 2
1682-1687

p.
1

IN THE NAME OF GOD AMEN. I JOHN ASHTON (blank) the County of Rappahannock FORD in Virginia, being of (blank) memory & knowing the frailties & uncertainties (blank) in this life doe make all other Wills formerly (blank) this to be my last Will and Testament this tenth (blank) 1675 Imprimis I resign my Soul to the hands of God my Creator hopeing & resting confidently that through his Mercie and the merritts of Jesus Christ my Redeemer I shall obtain pardon & remission for my manifold transgressions And to be made ptaker of those Joyes which are laid up for the Saints and Light my body I committ to the Earth to be buried with decensy and Christian buriall in expection that it with my Soule shall have a joyfull resurrection, As to my worldly Estate I dispose threof as followeth (vizt.)

I doe give and bequeath to my loveing Wife, ELIZABETH ASHTON, if she shall come over and dwel hereare all my Estate both personall & real during her life, But if she will not then doe I bind over my Estate to pay her Twenty pounds Sterl. p yeare or a hundred & fifty Sterl. which she wold rather have; I goe give five pounds Sterl. to THOMAS BUMBERY & his Wife and Twenty Shil. to Capt: JOHN ASHTON

I doe make my Brother, JAMES ASHTON, my whole Execulr. and the heires of his body forever, But in case he have none then after his decease to may Couzen, JOHN ASHTON, in Russell Street at the ADAM & EVE in LONDON & to his heires for ever

Signed Sealed and Deliver'd

in ye prsence of us DOMINICK RICE,   JOHN (Seal) ASHTON

ROBERT MASSESS

I the Subscribr: doe declare upon Oath that I saw JOHN ASHTON the above Testatr: Signe seale deliver promulg. & declare this to be his last Will and Testament

DOMINICK RICE

Juratus est RICE in Cur Com Rappa 6th die 7bris 1682

Test EDMD. CRASK, Cl Cur

Recordatr xx8 die Janry Anno 1682   Test EDMD. CRASK Cl Cur

pp.   Papers found in Mr. BEARBLOCKs Pocket Augt. 14th 1682
1-   RICHARD LEIGHTONs Bill to Mr. BEARBLOCK
2   DENIS EARLY by Bill
         ROBERT RUDDERFORD
         RICHARD WEST
         MR. DACRES Bill
         HENRY WHITEs Bill
         ARTHUR ONBY Bill
         JOHN WATSONs Bill
         ROBERT MOSS by Bill
         BRYAN WARD
         ROBERT ROSS an other Bill
         THOMAS SWINBORN
         CHARLES GOODRICH by Bill
         TOBIAS INGRAM
         NICHOLAS YATES
         DOCTR. SYNOCK
         Bill belonging to Majer PAUL WOODBRIDG

One Bill to Mr. MOORE & Mr. BEARBLOCK or either of them for
This is a Just Acct. of the Bill brought me out of Mr. BEARBLOCKs pockett 4th
Janry 1682

WILL. LLOYDS

Recordatr. xx die Janry Anno 1682

EDMD. CRASK Cl Cur

P Contra Creditr: in Tobos:
By Judgmt. agst ye Estate of WM. SHERRIT
By Judgmt. agst ye Estate of TIMOTHY KEISER
By Judgmt. to SAMLL. BRAT
They paid Mr. BAILY when SubSheriff for giving processions
By Judgmt. to JOHN ENGLISH for Smith's work of ye lifetime of ye JOHN BEAR-
BLOCK
By paid Clerks fees
By Charge in attending Court & Attorneys
Fee about the said Estate
Severall goods delivered to ALEXANDR. NEWMAN as they are apprized
By two Cowes & Calves delivd. to him
By one other Cow deliv'd him for BASSE
1679   By Appairil & wearing necessarys for JOHN NEWMAN
1680   By wearing Necessarys & apparril for him
By his owne & ye Soldir
1681   By apparrill & wearing necessarys
By his levy
By Ballr. of ye afore paymts. & dibinsmts. being 14434 Tob.
By what he paid in obtaining ye horse Dick sold by ALEXR. NEWMAN
By paid Mr. GLOVER for his paines & troubles taken abt. the Estate at the
request of JOHN and ALEXR. NEWMAN
By paid ANTHONY STEPTOE
By paid fouer barrells of Corn owing for before my possession

                                                                23539
By Bal due hereon   8466
June 15th 1682 Errors Excepted   32005
                    p me   PAUL WOODBRIDG
In Obeanunce to an order of Court, We the Subscribers have examined ye above
account & find due to the Estate of Mr. JOHN NEWMAN deced 8421 lbs. of Tobo., As witness
or: hands this 3d day of July 1682
April 20/   To 2 dowlls Shirts . . . 300   ALEXANDR. ☩ SWAN
    1682   To 2 pr of Stockings . 120   JOHN SAMPSON
             To one pr. shoes 133
                                       520
Recordt. xx6 die July Anno 1682

What I found about Mr. WM. BEARBLOCK body
2 small rings   1 pr Silver shoe buckles
1 great Ring   1 pr of old thread stockins
2 Swrt handchucheifs   a prob fowl pipe bowl
1 Ink horn   1 pr gloves
                                       1 Silver Case for little Sissors
                    REES EVANS

Juratus est EVANS 4th die Janry. in Cur Com Rappa: 1682
Recordtr. xx6 die Janry Anno 1682

p.   ESTAT of WILL. GRAY deced
2   is Dr.
    pd p order to GEORG JONES
    p Order to PETER DOWNMAN
    p order to Mr. MOSSELEY
    p. order to Mr. SYNOCK
    p order to Mr. RUSSELL
    p order to Mr. POOLE
    p pd. THO: INGRAM
    p pd PETER DOWNMAN
    Legacies paid out of the Estate
    p pd TOBY and THO. INGRAM one
    young mare
    p. ABNER GRAY one mare

Credtr. p Contra L Tob
p the Assisrrisemt.
p one Steer aged 4 years

Due to ye Orphans of GRAY
Errors Excepted p. JO. C. ALMOND
    ROBT. SYNOCK

28119

Recordtr. xx3 die Febry 1682

p.   THE INVENTORY of EDWARD DAVIS Estate
3   To one great Chest
    To one Small pott and hooks
    To one old Pallett
    To one old frying pan with a broken
    handle

To one old Sifter
To one old Smoothing Iron
To one old paile and other
    lumber

The above said Inventory & Apprismt. was made by us ye Subscribers: this 4th of Janry
1682

CHRISTOP: BLACKBORN
WM: GANNOCK

Recordatr. xx7 die Febry Ano 1682

pp.   IN THE NAME OF GOD Amen. I WILLIAM SERGENT being very sick and weake in
3-   body but of perfect minde & memory praised be God therefore doa make and or-
5   dayne this my last Will and Testament this 15th day of February A:DO: 16 (blank
    in manner following. Imprs. I give and bequeath my Soule to Almighty God my
Creator and Redeemer hoeping through the passion of Jesus Christ to enjoy Eternall
Salvation

It. I give & bequeath my body to the earth from whence it came to be decently buried
at the discretion of my Execuurs. hereafter named And as for what Worldly estate it hath
pleased God to bless me with I dispose thereof as followeth after my funerall charges
debts and Legacies pd. Revoaking all other and former Wills by me heretofore made

It. I give and bequeath unto my Sonn, GEORGE SERGENT, his heires and assignes for
ever all my lands wtsoever I have in Virga. or Elsewhere to be delivered to him by my
Execuutors named as soon as he shall attain to the age of Twenty yeares

Item I give and bequeath unto my said Sonn, GEORG, all my personall Estate soever togeather with the produce thereof to be delivered to him as soon as he shall attaine to
the age of Twenty yeares aforesaid

Item. My minde and Will is that if my Executors hereafter named shall think fitt to
bring my perishable goods to an appresiment or to be sold at an outcry then the pro-

duce thereof to be delivered to my said Son, GEORGE, at the age abovesd

It. My will and desire is that one diaper table Cloath, fifteen naplins, a bell mettle pot, a new Feather bed and furniture, ten breeding cowes, a bull and my mare remaine unsold with their encrease And that the said Cattle and Mares remain on the Plantation and land whereon I now live And with the encrease to be delivered to my said Son, GEORG, at the age aforesaid

It. My will is that what other goods my Executors hereafter named shall keep and feel fitt to be sold or apprised to Remaine in their custody and to be delivered to my sd Son, GEORG, at the age above said

It. My will is that out of ye pduce of what goods my Executors shall make sale of that it be laid out in good new houshold stuff and such other necessarys as they shall think fitt for the benefit of my said Son, GEORGE, and his Plantations And to be delivered to him at the age above said

Item. My will is that both my Plantations be kept employed by my Executors: and that the houses and fences be kept in Repaire until my said Son shall attaine to the age abovesaid and that one Sixty foot Tob. house be built on the Plantation where I now live about two yeares before he attaines to his said age

It. My will is that my Executors give a lease to RICHARD MATHEWS of the land he now lives on untill my sd Son comes to the age aforesd. he paying the quit rents during ye time

It. In case my said Son shall dye (wch. God forbid) before the attaines to the age of Twenty years aforesd, then I give unto RICHD. MATHEWS his heires and assignes forever ye Plantation where he now lives in the FORREST with a hundred acres of land adjoyning to it

It. In case of my Sons death abovesd, I give unto WILLIAM WHITRIDGE his heires and assignes for ever, Son of JOHN WHITRIDGE, one hundred acres of land of the same devident adjoyning on the dividing land between Mrs. JOANE CLARK and mine

It. In case of Sones death aforesaid, I give unto WILL WARREN his heires and assignes forever, Son of JOHN WARREN, one hundred acres of land of the same devident adjoyning on WILL WHITRIDGE, RICHARD MATHEWS & JOHN BOWER

It. In case of my Sones death aforesaid, I give unto HENRY FIELD, his heires and assignes forever, Son of ABRAHAM FIELD deced, one hundred acres of land of the same devident crossing the lines of WILL WHITLEDGE and WILLIAM WARREN to JOHN BOW-LERs line & back to the dividing line of Mr. JOHN CLARK and mine

It. In case of my Sones death aforesaid, I give unto WILL GRIFFIN his heires and assignes forever, Son of WILL GRIFFIN deced, fifty acres of land of the same devident beginning at the GREAT SWAMP of his Fathers line running along the said line to the line of HENRY FIELD aforesaid

Item. In case of my Sons death aforesd. I give unto FRANCIS STERNE, her heires and assignes forever, Daughter of DAVID STERNE, and REBECCAH WELLS, hir heires and assignes forever, Daughter of BARNABY WELLS, all the residue of the said land in the FORREST aforesaid to be equally devided between them quantity for quantity and quality for quality

It. In case of my Sons death aforesaid, I give unto JOHN DEANE his heires and assignes for ever, the Son of JOHN DEANE, one of my Executors hereafter named, all the Planta-tion with the land thereto belonging whereon I now live togeather with ten Cattle that is to say six Cowes one Bull and three Steers, Alsoe the hogs on the said land belonging to me

It. My will is that in case of my Sons death aforesaid, ye residue of my Estate to be dis-tributed among the poorest & most incapable of living of my God Children according to the discretion of my Executors if they think fitt

It. I give unto every and each of these my friends her named (Vizt) to GEORG JONES, to HONORIA his Wife, to JOHN WEIRE, to Mr. DANIELL GAMES, to Mr. THOMAS PERKINS, to Mrs. JANE DEANE, Wife to JNO. DEANE one of my Execors, to Mrs. MARTHA TAYLOR Twenty Shillings apeice to buy them mourning Rings

It. I give to each of my Executors hereafter named Twenty Shillings a piece to by them mourning Rings

Item My will is that my said Son remaine with his Godfather and Godmother untill he attaines to the age aforesaid, And to be brought up to learn to read write and cast accounts and the Grammer Rules if possible. And Lastly, I make ordaine and appoint Capt. GEORGE TAYLOR, Mr. JOHN DEAN JR., et Mrs. ELIZABETH JONES, Executors of this my last Will and Testament. In Testimony whereof I have sett my hand and fixed my Seale the date abovesaid

    ALEXR. DONIPHAN,   WILL SARGENT
    REES EVANS, JOHN MILLES

The Within named JOHN MILLS aged about 36 yeares doth depose and say that he did see the within named WILL SARGENT Signe Seale publish and declare this within written to be his last Will and Testament And that he was in perfect sence and memory at the Signing Sealing and publishing thereof As Witness my hand this 4th day of Aprill 1683
                JOHN MILLES

Juratus est MILLES in Cur Com Rappa: 4th die Aprilis Ao. 1683

The Within named ALEXANDR. DONIPHAN aged about 30 yeares doth depose and say the same as is above written As Witness my hand 13th day of Aprill 1583
                ALEXR. DONIPHANN

Juratus est DONIPHANN Coram me JON. STONE

REES EVANS aged about 30 yeares doth depose and say the same as is aboveaid
                REES EVANS

Probtr. p Sacrament et Recordatr. x4th die Aprillis Anno 1683
        Juratus Coram me CADWALLDR. JONES

pp.   IN THE NAME OF GOD Amen. I JOANE CLARK being sick & weake of boyd but of
5-   sound & perfect memory doe make this my last Will and Testament in manner
6   and form foll. Imprimis I bequeath my Soule to God that gave it And my body
(after Christian Burrial to the Grave in hopes that at the last Day my Body and Soule will be united and then through the merrits and by the Hand of my Blessed Lord Saviour Jesus Christ) I hope I shall be admitted into the Everlasting Kingdom of Heaven and as for my Temporall Estate that God hath been pleased to bestow upon & possess me with I bequeath as followeth:

Item I give unto my two Daughters, ANN GOWER and ELIZABETH JACOBUS, all my wearing appareell to be equally devided between them both

Item I give unto STANLY GOWER (the Sonn of FRANCIS and ANN GOWER) one Cow with all her increase forever to be deliverd to the said STANLEY the next Spring shall be a twelve month after my decease

Item I give unto ELIZABETH JACOBUS, Daughter of ANGELL JACOBUS & ELIZABETH, that Feather bed generally use to lye upon withe the boulster Rugg & two feather Pillows and I alsoe give unto the aforesaid Daughter of ANGELL JACOBUS one Cow with all her increase for ever to be delivered the next spring shall be a twelve month after my decease

Item I give unto my Sonn, JOHN CLARK, all other my Estate (Except what is above

specified) as houhould stuff and all other Hereditaments and likewise I give unto my
Sonn, JOHN CLARKE, all other my personall Estate as slaves, cattle hogs and a horse
called by the name of Button, And every thing else I die possest with whether debts or
otherwayes only what I above give to my Daughter and their Children excepted, But is
is my will that my sd Sonn, JOHN, remove nothing off from the Plantation I now live on
till he comes to the age of one and twenty

Item. I alsoe give to my Son, JOHN CLARK, a certaine tract of land that belongeth to me
of Seaven hundred ninety & two acres & one halfe acres that lyeth upwards neare
RAPPA RIVER & nigh unto Mr. WILLIAM SARGENT to him my said Sonn and his heires
for ever, but if my said Sonn should die without issue then the said Tract of land to be
equally divided between the heires of the bodies of my two Daughter, ANN GOWER and
ELIZABETH JACOBUS

Item I do make & constitute my Sonne JOHN CLARK my whole and said Executor, my
debts being first paid

Item I give unto FRANCIS GOWER, Son of FRANCIS and ANN GOWER, one Cow to be delivered the next Spring come twelve month after my decease the wch Cowe I give with
its increase for Ever It is to be understood that this Cow likewise is to be excepted from
those Cattle I give to my Son, JOHN, as well as the other two I gave to my Grand Children
STANLY GOWER and ELIZABETH JACOBUS; I doe likewise desire my trusty and welbeloved
friend, Coll. JOHN STONE of Rappae: County to guide direct & oversee my Sonn, JOHN
CLARK, being young till he come to ye age of one and twenty And this my last Will &
Testament makeing void all former wills I have hereunto sett my hand & Seale this
eight day of March One thousanD six hundred Eighty & two
Signed & Sealed in ye prsents of
    EDMUND NORTHEN,   JOAN CLARKE
    WILLIAM WARD, THOMAS X HART
    EDMUND NORTHEN aged about thirty years and WILLIAM WARD aged about twenty
eight years doth depose & say that they did see the abovenamed Mrs. JOANE CLARK signe
Seale & declare this to be her last Will & Testament and that she was in perfect sence
and memory at the signing hereof As Witness or: hands this 3d day of May 1683
                                            EDMUND NORTHEN
                                            WILLIAM WARD

    Jurati sun NORTHEN et WARD in Cur Com Rappae 3d die May ano 1683
    Probatr p Sacrament et Recordatr 9th die Maii ano 1683

pp.   Rappae: An Account of what goods were sold at an OUTCRY or part of the
6-   May 12th   Estate of WM. SARGENT deced according to his last Will and Testa-
7   1683   ment and Judgments confessed into Security before us ye Sub-
                     scribers as followeth (Vizt.) DANIELL BORNE confessed Judgmt.
WILLIAM TARRANTs Security To one Cow & Calfe at 600 Tobo:
JAMES SEATES confessed Judgmt. DANL: BORNE Security
    To red heifer & a black heifer & a black pied bull
JOHN MILLS confessed Judgmt. Capt. GEO: TAYLOR Security
    To 4 Steers 2 yrs. 1/2 old a peice
JAMES SCOTT confessed Judgmt. JAMES TRENT Security
    to 2 young red Steers & one black Bull
DANIELL MALLETT confessed Judgmt. WILL PAYNE Security
    To one Brown Steere
JOHN WOOD confessed Judgment and DANIELL SHIPLEY Security
    to 1: 3 yeare old Steer one yearling Bull & 1: heifer

JAMES SCOTT confessed Judgment JAMES TRENT Security
    to 2 Cowes at 1070
BARNABY WELLS confessed Judgment (blank) Security
    to 2 Steers about 7 yeares old
JOHN QUIZENBORGH confessed Judgmt. Mr. HUMPHREY POPE Security
    to red yearling heifer
GEORGE SOUTHEN confessed Judgment. JOHN BATES Security,
    to one horse & 7500 bricks
FRANCIS STERNE confessed Judgmt. DAVID STERNE Security
    to a paire of wheels
JOHN WARRIN confessed Judgmt. JOHN WILLIAM Security
    to a parcell of Cloaths
JOHN MILLS confessed Judgmt. Capt. GEO: TAYLOR Security
    to a pcell of Pewter & Iron Pot
JOHN RICHARDS confessed Judgmt. JAMES GREDIT Security
    To a parcell of Pewtr. & an Iron pott
Mr. ALEXR. DONIPHAN confessed Judgmt. JAMES TRENT Security
    to a parcell of Pewter & a r of Andirons
RICHARD MATHEWS confessed Judgmt JOHN MOTLEY Security
    to goods bought
JOHN MOTLEY confessed Judgmt. JAMES TRENT Security
    to a parcell of goods
Mr. EDMUND CRASK Security for Mr. HENRY AWBREY confessed Judgmt.
    to Goods
Doctr. SYNOCK confessed Judgment. RICHARD BRAY, Security
    to his Debts
Mr. RICHARD BRAY confessed Judgmt. Doctor SYNOCK security
    to his Debts
ROBERT GAMES confessed Judgmt. JOHN SMITH Security
    to a Bed
Mr. EDMUND CRASK confessed Judgmt. Mr. HENRY AWBREY Security
    to a parcell of Pewter
Mr. RICHARDS confessed Judgment (blank) Security
    for bucks

                  HENRY AWBREY   Quorum
                  SAML. BLOMFIELD   Justices

Recordtr. Test   EDMD. CRASK, Cl Cur.

pp.   IN THE NAME OF GOD Amen I JOHN MILLS being very sick & weak of body but
7-   prfect of Sence but I doe bequeath my Soule to the Lord And my body to be de-
8   cently buried in hopes of Resurrection to life eternall: And I doe give and be-
      queath to my Son, ROBERT MILLS, one hundred & fourty acres of land bounding
upon a DEEP SWAMP joyning upon ANTHONY NORTH excepting the NIMCOCK VALLEY
and ye North side of the Valley which I doe reserve for my two younger Sonns for
Timber and I doe give to my Son, JOHN MILLS, one hundred and fourty acres of land
bounding upon his Brother, ROBERT, above written, And the remaining of the said Devident I leave to be equally divided between the two younger Brothers, HENRY MILLS
and JAMES MILLS and if either of the younger Brothers should decease this prsent
world without issue from either of their own bodys ye Survivr. of either of them to

have all the land to himselfe

And I doe give to my two Daughters, MARTHA and JANE, one heifer a peice and if either of the said heifers should dy without increase they are to be made good out of the Stock,

And I doe give to the above said JAMES MILLS one yearling Cow calf of the breed of the Cow called Cherry,

And I do give one cow to the above said HENRY MILLS and he is to take his Choice out of the Stock,

And I do give to the two younger Brothers one Mare and her increase betwixt them,

And I doe give to the two youngest Brothers one Feather Bedd betwixt them both but they are not to take it out of the house as long as the abovesaid JAMES MILLS doth stay with his Mother,

And I doe make my Wife whole Executrix This my last Will and Testament. As Witness my hands and Seale this 5th of March 1682/3

Teste   JOHN KINGE.   JOHN ✕ MILLS
        JOHN ROBERTS
        WILL ᴍ MACKENNY

JAMES KING aged 26 yeares or thereabouts sworn saith that he did see the within named JOHN MILLS Signe Seale publish & declare the within written as his last Will & Testament and that he was in perfect sence and memory to the best of the Deponents knowledge

                                                       JOHN KING

JOHN ROBERTS aged 38 yeares or thereabout sworne said the same as JOHN KING
                                                       JOHN ROBERTS

WILLIAM MACKENNY aged 60 years or thereabouts sworne saith the same as JOHN KING
                                                       WILLIAM MACKENNY

Probatr p Sacrament et Recordatr xx6th die Junii Anno 1683

pp.   RAPPA: COURT. An Inventory of the Estate of THOMAS ROBERTS late of sd County
8-   deced as it was taken vallued and apprized by us
9
                                                       JOHN JONES
                                                       ANTHONY SMITH
                                                       RICHARD GREENSTED

By vertue of an Order of the said County Court the 25th Aprill 1683
Imprs. One mare and yearly Colt in Tob:
        It. one gelding horse
        It. three Cowes & Calves, one Cow with Calf & one yearly
        It. four two yeare olds
        It. one Cow about 10 yeares old not seen or apprized
        It. one man Servt. named CARNOUGH McKENNY about 2 1/2 yrs. to serve
        It. one boy Servt. named GRIFFETH RIDGE 8 yrs to Serve 10 mo.
        It. one litle cask & two milk trays
        One old Couch bed bolster rug & blankett
        a prcell of pewter
        a small iron pott & pott hooks
        a frying pan
        one piggin & pale
        It. 6 old Chaires & an old Sadle
        It. one Smoothing Iron heaters six shovell & tongs
        It. one small Dantflick Case & bottles

It. the deceased wearing apparrell

It. a parcell of Table linen two old towells & 2 pillows cs.

It. one case of Pistolls ye one unfixed old holsters & bress plate

It. a parcell of Old Books

It. an old Chess & an old Trunk

It. an old Cart and wheels

It. One Feather bed bolster 2 pillows two blanketts & one rugg with callico
hangings & a small callico carpitt

Bills in the name of the Deced (Vizt.)

JAMES LAND for 420; THO: WHEELER for 400; RICE FLEEPE for 500; ANDREW DODING for 69; MARY DAY for 200; THOMAS GAMES for 429; in all Two thousand & eighteen pounds Tob.

It. a parcell of goods as pr: Invoyce eight pounds one Shill: nine pence Sterl. And Bills of Exchang. for Twenty five pounds ten Shill. Sterl. protested

This Inventory taken by us whose names are subscribed Amounted to Thirteen thousand eight hundred & eighteen pounds of Tob. besides a parcell hand packed in a hhd. and thirty three pounds Eleaven Shill. Nine pence Sterl. mony.

Witness or: hands this 25th Aprill 1683 aforesaid

Sworn ye day and year aforesaid

before me HENRY WILLIAMSON

JOHN JONES
ANTHO: SMITH
RICHD. GRINSTED

Recordatr. xx7 die Junii Anno 1683

pp.   Friday 13th Aprill 1683
9-   AN INVENTORY and Apprisemt. of the Estate of WILL SARGENT deced apprized
10   by us ye Subscribers as fol:
Imprs.   In the Hall

22 yards of Nar: blew at 7; 1 Ell of dowlis ragg end; 4 Ells 1/2 of ditto 16; 12 Ells wt. Ozenbridge 9; 26 yds 2/4 Linsey Wooley 10; 7 yard red Cotton 12; 65 lb. Pewter at 10: p lb; 11 lb old ditto 10 lb p. 5 pewter plates, 1 small bason, 11 porrings, 3 Sawsers, 1 larg salt celler, 1 small ditto; 1 good candletstick, 1 bad ditto; 2 quart potts; 2 old chamber potts; 3 old Tankards, one old Flaggon; 1 old Cup, 1 tin drugding box, one old yarn Rugg. one Feathr. bed boulster & pillow & one pr sheet; one Coat jacket & breech; one pr. new yarn hose, 2 pr old; 1 pr. boys yarn hose, 1 pr mens ditto; 1 new Bridle & Sadle. 1 pr. small Stiliards. a parcell of old Cloaths, 1 small looking glass, 3 old dimity west coats & a pr of Drawers; 2 old towells & old pillow Cover. 1 table cloath; 1 Callico Neck Cloath, 1 new Stript ditto; 1 small seilskin Trunk; 1 box wth horse medicines; 2 old Chests, 1 chess of Drawrs: and a Calicos Cubbard Cloath; 1 new Table & forme, 1 small table. 2 high Chaires wooden & two ditto; 1 new bedstead

In ye Kitchin

a table & formes, 5 milk trays, 2 wooden plattrs; 6 tin panns, 1 iron kettle, 3 iron potts. 2 shoe horns, Iron driping pan; 1 old brass kettle & Skillett, 1 grid iron; 2 pr Tongs, 1 fire Shovell, 1 box Iron & heaters; 1 spitt, 1 pr. andirons, 1 old pestell, 1 iron ladle & flesh fork, 1 brass Skimr., 1 small slice, 2 pr. pot racks; 1 frying pan, 1 old carving knife, 1 fixed gun, 1 gun without a lock, 1 hold beard; 4 old payles, 1 old flock bed 2 boulsters 1 rugg and a pr of blanketts; one old flock bed & rugg. one old brass mortar & pestell. one old tin funnell

in his SMITH's SHOPE

1 larg grind-stone; 1 Anvill & 2 fice iron; 1 Sledg & vice. 1 pr Smiths bellows; 23 lb of Steel & 26 lb of other Steel, a parcell of new iron; 2 chaldrons 1/2 of Cole; 1 scroll plate

& tapps; 22 Tiles; Sledges hamrs. & ye rest Tools; Servt. woman 2 yrs. Serv., a kline of bricks;

Milk House

1 old Powdring Tubb; 1 little Table; 1 parcell of old Books, 1 Cart & wheels

The Cattle

2 yearly bulls, 1 heifr; 2 draft oxen, 4 steers, 3 year old a paice; 3 steers 3 yeares old, 4 steers two yeares old; 2 heifers 3 yeares old, 3 old cows & 1 calfe; 13 year old Bull, 1 yearly old; 1 Steer 4 year old; 1 Steer 3 years old, 1 gray horse

IN OBEDIENCE to an ord. of the Worshipfll. Court of Rappa: bearing date ye 4th day of April 1683, we ye Subscribers have apprized according to ye best of or: Judgmt. ye Estate of WILL SARGENT deceased what was presented to or: veiw by the Executr. thereof, which ammounteth to the sum of Three and Twenty thousand and eight hundred & sixty three pounds of tobacco

Juratur coram me
    13th Aprilis 1683
        JON: STONE
    Recordatr. Test   THO: NEW Dept. Cl Cur

GEORGE JONES
DAVID D STERNE
FRANCIS $\underline{I}$ STERNE

pp.   AN ACCOT. of Mr. RICHARD HOBBS Estate Inventories & valued June ye 14th 1683
10-   Imprs. 4 Oxen
        4 Steers, 4 yeare old apeice
        1 Bull of 3 yeares old
        1 Bull of 2 yeares old
        9 Cows & 9 Calves 500 pr
        2 Cows without Calves
        1 Trundell bedsted, 1 Flock bed and Boulster, 1 rugg & feather pillows, one
            blankett
        One Chaff Bed & boulster, 1 rug & two pillows
        a small parcell of earthen ware
        One Sheete & Canvis Table cloath & old table cloath, 11 napkins & towells
        5 2 year old heiffers
        3 Cow yearlings
        a Feild of Standing Wheat
        4 Mares, 1 yearly Colt 2 Mare fold
        6 Ewes 6 lambs & 2 rams
        The stock of hoggs
        1 pr small Stilliards
        3 pr. mens yarn stockins
        3 pr Irish Stockins
        1 pr Ticken boddese
        a prcell of Sorry lace
        1 lb. of black thread & pcell of silk
        1 pr Childrens hose & red galoom
        3 ells of Flaxen Cloath
        2 yards wt: Callicoe
        2 gunns & 2 yds. 1/4 of Dimity
        7 yds 1/2 of fine Seirdge
        3 yds 1/4 of Flannew
        a pcell of Crist Cutt
        6 Turkey work Chaires, 5 leathr. ditto

1 pt. lardg. Andirons and one great table and form
1 side Cubbard & small table
2 Rettermaster Carpitts and 3 bushells of Salt
1 flock bed & boulster 1 pr of blanketts, 1 greenrugg, 1 bed sted
1 pr. Rettermastr. Cortins & valiane;
1 Feather bed, 1 Chattayl boister, 1 pr Canvas Sheets, 1 pr blankts., & rugg,
        2 standing bedsted, 1 sett curtains & vallians & chimney cloath
2 Iron Skitts & 1 doz. of new pewter spoons
a prcell of old Pewtr., 1 gal. pewtr. pots
2 frying panne & pr of Iron tongs
1 pr bellows & two candle sticks
2 iron potts 1 gridiron, 1 smooth iron
1 brass kettle
2 plows & Irons
4 plow Chaines & a Jack
1 table, 1 wooden chair & fristell
1 little brass kettle & skimer & a flesh fork
3 old axes & 3 wedges
hooks for pots
1 old chair an old Couch & old Sadle
10 Sherlocks old panns earth panns
1 Earthen Buttr. pott.
2 larg Slaughter hides
1 small coverled & spade
a parcell old Sidir casqe & 2 Sifters
1 Sadle bridle & sadle cloath
2 pr of boots & spurrs
1 pr Slip leathrs. bridle stirup iron & one girt
1 pr of old wool cards brass scales & weights
2 razors 1 iron ketch & built. moulds
3 old Oagers, 1 cross-cut saw & 9 reap hooks
Rop and Wool a new weeding hoe & a lardg knife
2 pr dimity drawer. 1 westcoate and a closs bodied coate
1 rideing coate & trouses, two shirts & pr of drawrs.
1 Course holland Shirt & 3 yds of Lockerrim
1 pr Holland Stockins & pr Sleeves, a parcell of thread and a parcell of
        course linen cut out
2 lb. thread & a few blew prints
a Knife & fork & a razor
3 chests, 2 boxes & a trunk
3 bushells Salt at Coll. LOYDs.
1 Servt. boy 6 months to Serve
1 New England buckett & an old pale, 6 old pewter plates, 6 new pewt. plates,
        1 punch pewter bason
An old chest of Iron lumber
one pr iron Spancells
one flock bed, 2 pillows, 1 rugg, a blankett
1 powdering tubb
3 bridles & an old Sadle
One boate 16 foot p keell

One cart & wheeles
One bill of ANGELL JACOBUS
One bill of ROBERT TOMLIN JUNR.
One bill of RICHARD GREEN

Suma Totalis   44339

ROBERT SISSEN   FRANCIS POWER
WILLIAM DAWSON   ROBERT TOMLIN JUNR.

The Apprisemt. & RICHARD GREEN, Adminstr., were sworn before me this 13th of June
1683 by vertue of an order of Rappa. Court

WILL LLOYD

Recordatr. xx3 die July Ano 1683
Teste THOS: NEW Dept. Cl Cur

p.   INVENTORY of ye Estate of JOB THOMAS deced his Wife alsoe al ye same time
12   died & now in ye possession of Mr. JOHN SUGGETT Febbry. 27th 1682/3
        Imprs. 4 porrigrs; 4 spoones, 1 frying pan; 1 Crupe felt, a pockett Bible, 3 old
Petticoats, 2 new lockt., in Shiffts; a womans wastecoates, some old waring linnen of ye
mans and womans scarce valuable, 1 old pr Sattin boddes, 1 pr of other boddes, severall
pcells thread; 2 pr yarn stockins, 1 pr of gloves 1 pr of Shoes; a Shoat more; 1 pale, 2
small geldings, 1 Silvr. brakin; 17 peices woman lyning, 2 parcells of woolen yarn; 32
lb. dryed beefe; one Kerzy wastcoat and drawers wch ye yt. STRIPT had for his paines &
making ye grave, one chest trunck, some other trifles not worth naming, ye whole
Intrust not worth much

Testes: WM. SLOUGHTER

& Bushells of Corne, his 1/3 of 6 shoates, 1 doz. poultrey
   In Obedience to an Ordr. of the Worll. Court of Rappa. County bearing date ye 7th of
March 1682/3 we whose names are within written have apprized ye Estate of JOB THO-
MAS deceased as witness our hands this 5th of Aprill 1683
Aprill ye 5th 1683   ALEXANDR. SWAN
                              DENIS   1683   McCARTY

Sworn before me Mr. JOHN SUGGETT, Admr.
 & Mr. ALEXANDR. SWAN & Mr. DENIS CARTY
Aprizors   SAML. PEACHEY
Recordatr xx3 die July Anno 1683
                 Teste THOMAS NEW Deputy to EDMOND CRASK Cl Cur

pp.   IN THE NAME OF GOD Amen. I EDMOND CRASK of County of Rappa. being in a
12-   sick and weak condition but of perfect minde and memory Blessed be God there-
13   fore, doe hereby make and ordaine this to be my last Will and Testament in
        manor. & form following.
Imprs. I give & bequeath my sould to Almighty God who gave it me and my body to ye
Earth to be decently burried at the discretion of my Executrs. hereafter named.
   Item I will that ELIZABETH MOSS and FRANCES MOSS be paid their equall shares of their
deceased Fathers Estate according to ye terme of the Inventory & Apprismt. out of my
Estate by my Executors hereafter named
   Item. I give unto my well beloved Wife, ELIZABETH, one Negro (blotted out) and my
mourning ring to hir & hir heires forever (blot) my Son, JOHN CRASK, one young
negro boy called Michall & my sword and belt to him & his heires forever
   I give to my Daughter, ELLEN CRASK, one young Negroe girle called Jenny and her
own Mothers Cabbinett to her and her heires forever

Item I give unto my Son, JOHN, aforesaid a tract of land containing Six hundred & fifty acres being part of the Devident formerly belonging to Mr. THOMAS BUTTON deceased called the RANG wch. was lately granted to me by Escheat to him and his heires forever

Item I give to my Daughter, ELLEN, a tract of land containing Three hundred acres lying near to the said RANG land wch. I purchased of ROBERT & GEORGE PLAY to her & her heires for ever

Item All ye rest of my personall Estate of what nature or kind soever it be I give & bequeath to my welbeloved Wife, ELIZABETH, & to my Son, JOHN, aforesaid, and to my Daughter, ELLEN, to be equally devided between them

Item I make & ordaine my loveing Wife, ELIZABETH, and my Son, JOHN, Executrix and Executr. of this my last Will & Testament and I doe desire my hnred. Friends, Lieut. Coll. WM. LOYD and Mr. HENRY AWBREY, to be assisting to them in advising them in the Management of my Estate, And I doe give to each of them a mourning Ring of Fifteen shillings price for their paines & care And likewise I desire the Worshipl. Court of Rappak: to be aideing & assisting my Wife & Children for the procuring what Clerks fees shall be due to me in this County of Rappae: or else where; And what the Sheriffs shall be disscient in Collecting I humbly desire that they will give a power to THOMAS NEW to collect the Tobo. that shall be found due to me and pay the Debts; And use means possibly he can the recovery of them, And for what Tob: he shall soe collect and pay, he to receive his full Sallery for the same, he paying to my sd Executrs. the remainder in ye County of Rappae: Revoaking all other Wills by me formely made I declare and pronounce this to be my last Will and Testament

In Witness whereof I have hereunto sett my hand and affixed my Seale this 20th day of July Anno Dom 1683

Signed Sealed declared & published
in the presence of us HENRY ⟂ NEWLON,   EDMUND CRASK
        THOMAS HERBERT, THO: NEW

I the above named HENRY NEWLON aged about 29 yeares do depose and say that I did see the above named Testator Signe Seale publish and declare this above written to be his last Will and Testament and that he was in perfect sence and memory at ye signing & sealing hereof to ye best of yor: deponents knowledg. and further saith not

                                        HENRY ⟂ NEWLON

Wee the abovesd THO: HERBERT & THO: NEW do depose & say the same as before mentioned as further saith not   THO: HERBERT
                                        THO: NEW

Probatr. p Sacrament HEN. NEWLON, THO: HERBERT et THO: NEW in Cur Com Rappa. prima die August Anno 1683

Test THO: NEW Cl Cur et Recordatr. x4th die August 1683

pp.   February ye 16th 1679
13-   IN THE NAME OF GOD Amen. the last Will & Testament of SYMON MILLER of the
15   Freshes of Rappa aged Seaven and thirty yeares or thereabout being of true and
       perfect memory doe in the first place commit my Soule unto God as a Mercifull
Creator relying upon Jesus Christ my Redeemer by whose precious blood I hope to be saved, I commit my Body to the arth to be decently buried I doe will and bequeath as followeth

Item I give unto my Sonn, SYMON MILLER, halfe the devidend of land I now live on to him and his heires for ever And my Son, SYMON MILLER, to cleare and plant as he shall think fitting in his Mothers Life time upon the said Devidend excepting the Plantation, And Further I give to my Son, SYMON, a sorrill Mare with a white blaze on the face & all her Increase to him forever. And in case I dye it is my will that my Son, SYMON, be sent the next yeare for England

Item I will and bequeath to my Sonn, WILLIAM MILLER, the other halfe dividend of land to him and his heires forever & a Chessnut Mare with her Increase forever and full power I give to my Son, WILLIAM MILLER, to clear & plant as he shall think fitting upon any part of the said devidend

Item I give unto my Son, JOHN MILLER, Two hundred acres of land adjoyning to DOC-TOR REYNOLDS to him and his heires forever And a black Mare with a hook brand on the near buttock with her increase forever

Item I give unto my Daughter, SUSANNA MILLER, Fouwer hundred eight acres & a halfe of land being the halfe devidend of land adjoyning to Col. CADWALLDR. JONES on the head of PUMANS INN to her and her heires forevr.

And my old Mare with her Increase for ever

Item. I give to my Daughter, ISABELLA MILLER, the other halfe of the Devidend at PUMANS INN to her & her heires for ever, and a black Mare about two yeares old and her increase forever, the Mare is branded with 𝔖𝔐 on her neare buttock

Item I give unto my Daughter, MARGARET MILLER, Two hundred acres of land on ye back of my land adjoyning to DOCTOR REYNOLDS to her and her heires for ever and a brown Mare branded 𝔖𝔐 with her increase for ever

And Last of all I leave my Wife full Executrx. and the rest of my Estate I give my Wife to bring up my Children and to be at her disposing after my decease my Debts and other Necessary charges being paid, And in case my Wife dy before she maryeth the rest of my Estate to be devided equally betwixt my chIdren.

It is my will that the three Mares given to my Son, WILL & my Son JOHN & my Daughter SUSAN that the foales they go with all shall goe into the Stock and if any of them being a Mare foale it is to be given to my Wifes Son, ANTHONY PROSSER, and if they doe not bring a Mare foale my Wife as she thinks fitting is to dispose of so much of the Stock to purchase her Sonn, ANTHONY, a mare foale, And all the male Increase of all the Mares, Except my Son, SYMONs, to goe into ye said former Stock till my Children come to the age of Fourteen, then male & female of the Children to have ye full increase and if any of these children dy before they come of lawfull age then that Estate land or mares to be equally devided among the Survivors and if any of the Childrens mares dy then my Wife is to by out of the said Stock to make good the same

And to the Sons of Mr. PROSSER every one of them are to have a heifer delivered to them one after another when they come to Eighteen yeares of age to be delivered by my Executors after my decease

Item I give unto my Wife, MARGARET MILLER, the Plantation and houses I now live in during her naturall life, And in case she should mary one that should lett the house and Orchard goe to Ruin, then she is to return to her thirds according to Law, And I make JAMES ASHTON Overseer over my Estate & Children and the said Overseer, JAS. ASHTON, to dispose of the said Children at sixteen yeares of age as he shall think fitt but in case the said Mr. JAMES ASHTON dyeth then the Children to be at their own disposing if they like to goe to any handy craft trade they have a mind unto

Sealed and delivered in the presence of us

NATHANIELL TOMLIN,   SYMON MILLER
FRANCIS THORNTON,
JAMES TAYLOR

Mr. FRANCIS THORNTON aged about 32 yeares or thereabouts saith that on Febby. 18th 1679 was at the house of Capt. SYMON MILLERs and he then and there called me into his inner roome & presented this Will to me and said it was his Will wch. accordingly I witnessed it further saith not.

FRANCIS THORNTON

Juratus est THORNTON in Cur Com Rappa. quinto die 7bris Anno. 1683
Test THO: NEW Cl Cur p temr.

I the Subscriber doe hereby testifie and declare that I did see the within Testar. signe seale & publish this wthin mentioned to be his last Will & Testament and that he was then in perfect sence and memory to the best of mthis Deponts. knowledg And further saith not

JAMES TAYLOR

Juratus est TAYLOR in Cur Com Rappa. 7 die Maii Ano 1684
Probatr. p Sacrament Recordatr. xx2 die May Ano. 1684
Test WM. COLSTON Cl Cur

p. RAPPA. COUNTY
15   Whereas DOMCK. RICE this day make information unto us that JAMES PRITCHARD being tenant to ye sd DOMINICK RICE & debt for his Rent now three yeares rent past of wch. was to be pa. in Tob: & part in Corne, the Plantacon of the sd RICE now left by the said PRITCHARD wth the Crop of Tob: & Corn made thereon &c.

These are therefore in his Maties name to Authoriz Mr. DOMCK. RICE to enter upon the sd Plantation & take care of what is lwft upon the Plantation togeather wth the Corn and Tob: he the said RICE taking care to Inventory ye Estate Mr. ALEXANDR. SWAN & Mr. DENIS CARTY are hereby required to pform & take an Inventory thereof & make re-port to the next Court Mr. RICE being justly paid his Rent there are two Attachmts. already issued, the one to TIMOTHY BARNS, ye other to JNO. PEACOCK being dated Novbr. 6th Instant. Given undr. or: hands Novbr. 10th 1682

SAML. PEACHEY
WM. SLAUGHTER

In Obedience to the wthin prcept we whose names are undr: written have Inventories as fol: this 13th 9ber 1682

Imprs. 12 barrells of Indian Corn, 1 Sow & 4 Shoates, 1 small iron pot contd. 3 quarters 3 hangers, 1 small frying pan, 1 old small Ches & one little box, 1 small sifting tray, 2 bushells of beans, 1 bushell of Salt, 1 small powdring Tubb & old couch & bedsted; 1 old hilling hoe & hamer; 1 runlett, 3 gall. 1 old ax, 1 old table very small; 1 prcell of Tob. hanging;   Suma totis 2372

Pd. out of ye sd Corn for the gathering to ye Neighbors to RICHD. APPLEBY for 3 days work; To JNO. PEACOCK ditto; to THOM: BARNE 4 daies; to 9 days my own folks

ALEXANDER SWAN
DENIS CARTY

Aprismt. 2372 Tobo: 415 Rest due to Estate 1957
Recordatr. xx4th die 7bris Ano 1683
Test THO: NEW Cl Cur p Temp.

p. AN INVENTORY of ye Estate of WM. ROBINSON apprized by us whose names be
16   undr. written being appointed by ye Worshipfull Court of Rappa. & as it was
     brought to us by JOHN BURCH this 26th March 1678

To 2 Cowes of 7 & 8 yeares old; To 2 heifers 3 years old; To heifer year & halfe old, To 4 yearlin, To a bedstead, To one low bedstead; To a table & forme, To 2 chaires, To one old chest, To a Cattaile bed & blankett, To 5 pewter dishes & plates, To 6 old trays, old butter tub, old sifter, 3 wedges & hand saw, old paile not worth anything   2772

The abovesaid is apprized by us to ye best of or: judgments & knowledg by us
                    ALEXR. DONIPHAN
                    JAMES ᛏ TRENT

pp.   AN INVENTORY of the Estate of JOHN MORRAH deced as the same was exhibited on
16-   Oath of Mr. THO: CHITTY & KATHERIN his Wife unto us whose names are hereunto
17   subscribed and apprized by us on oath according to an Ordr. of Cort. for that
        purpose & taken on the 16th day of July 1683 & are as fol. (Vizt.)
                Bills and Books Debts
        RICHARD JESPER p Bill; EDMD. THOMAS p book; RICHD. PEACOCK by bal. of Accot.
pork: GILES WEBB; ROGER WATERS, Mr. JNO. BAYLEY, JOHN JACOB, HENRY AUSTIN, Mr.
DENIS CARTY, JOHN HAWKINS, THO: WILKS, HENRY WILSON, THOS: CHITTY, SAML.
WHITHEAD, ROBT. BAYLEY JUNR., EDWD. LEWIS ALEXR. DUDLEY, WM. BARBER, RICHD.
KING p Bill; RODDRICK JONES Bill; THO: GEORG   Pork 225   8158
 These Debts are entered in R. Book wrot p me JNO. BALY & remains yet in Mr. CHITTYs
. possession
 In Mony; In NEW ENGLAND mony; SPANISH money & pieces of eight; one halfe peice,
one quarter peice, Seaven yards & a halfe of Scotch Cloath, two old neck Cloath, a
napkin, pr gloves, a Rasor & an old bagg. These things are in a Chest with a lock. The
money & the goods abovementioned are yet in the hands of Mr. THO: CHITTY.
 The apparrell of the deced both linen woolen hose shoes batts & hammock Scotch pladd
& Irish gaddoo
 July 16th 1683 Sworn before me Mr. GILES WEBB as alsoe Mr. THO: CHITTY &
KATHERINE his Wife for the discovery of his Estate of the above sd MORRAH & Mr.
ALEXR. SWAN and DENIS CARTY apprissers
                    SAMLL. PEACHEY   ALEXANDR. SWAN
                                                  DENIS MACARTY
Recordatr xx6 die Septembr. ano 1683

pp.   IN YE NAME OF GOD Amen, I JOHN MORRAH being sick in body but of perfect
17-   mind and memory doe make this my last Will and Testament as fol: disanulling
18   all formr. Wills by me made.
        Imprs. I doe bequeath my soul to God who gave it me, hoping in Jesus Christ my
Mediatr. for salvation at the last day and in him only doe I put my trust, with my body to
convenient Christian burial
 Item. I give to my Godson, THOMAS WARDON of BARBADOES One thousand pounds of
Muscovada Sugar, which Sugar is in ye hands of JOSEPH WARDON of BARBADOES, Father
of the said THOMAS
 Item. I give to THOMAS CHITTY JUNYOR One thousand pounds of good sound Tobacco
 Item. I give to JOHN JACOB my broad Cloath Coate & breeches
 Item. I give to my good friend, GRACE BEDFORD, one thousand pounds of good sound
tobacco
 Item. I doe ordr. and appoint my good Friends, THOMAS CHITTY SENIR and JOHN
BAYLEY. to be my only Execrs. and doe give all the remaining part of my estate to them.
 In Witness hereunto sett my hand and seale this fourteenth day of Septembr. in the
year of or: Lord God 1682
Recordatr. test   THO: NEW Cl Cur p Tempre
 The Depostion of Mr. DOMINICK RICE aged aboute thirty three yeares or thereabouts
saith that being sent for from my hom to the house of JOHN JACOB & found JOHN MOR-

RAH very sick & lying in a couch. I asked him how he did & he the sd JOHN MORRAH gave answer that he was very ill at wch time Mr. JOHN BAYLEY brought to the said MORRAH his Will in writing & read the same to ye sd MORRAH distinctly deliberately word by word who answered very well & said he was ready to Signe it and accordingly endeavoured to rise up & to signe the same but was at that time advised to the contrary by his Nurs, he being then in a great sweat, wch. sd Will to the best of yr. deponts. memory is the very memorial paper now exhibited to this Worshipfull Court by Mr. JOHN BAYLEY and Mr. THOMAS CHITTY and farther this Depont. saith not

DOMINICK RICE

NICHO. CUNSTABLE aged 44 years or thereabouts sworne and examined saith that being sent for to the house of Mr. JOHN JACOB did here the said Will read distinctly to JOHN MORRAH who approved of it in every respect above mentioned And deposeth the same above mentioned & further saith not

NICHO. ⃝ CONSTABLE

The Deposition of RODERICK JONES aged about thirty five saith that JOHN MORRAH being at my house about ye midle time of June last said he had a Will made wch wanted nothing but signing, And that it was his last Will & Testament, And further saith not

RODERICK R ╪ JONES

Jurati sunt DOMINICK RICE et CONSTABLE et RODERICK JONES in Cur Com Rappa 8th die Septembris Anno 1683

Probatr. p Sacramt Coram Recordatr. xx6 die Septembris 1683

pp.   IN THE NAME OF GOD Amen the Seventeenth day of August Anno Dom 1683 I THO-
18-   MAS GEORG of the County of Rappae in Virginia Gent. being sick and weak in
19   body but of sound mind & memory (praised be God) doe therefore make and declare my last Will & Testamt. in maner and form following (Vizt.)

First & principally I recomend my Soul back into the hands of the Almighty and my body I comitt into the earth to be decently buried at the Discreation of my Deare Wife, trusting and assuridly believeing it shall partake of that Glorious Resurrection pur-chased by that precious blood & meritts of or; dear Lord & Saviour Jesus Christ And as for the worldly Estate God of his goodness hath blessed me wth. after my Debts paid and funerall charges discharged, I dispose thereof as herein is specified (That is to say)

I give and bequeath unto my Son, LEROY GEORG, my horse called Sutt with all the fur-niture I have belonging to a mans horse, together with all my books

Item. I give and bequeath unto my said Daughter, MARGARET, Twenty thousand pounds of Toba: & cask to be paid her by my Executors hereafter named or the land I purchased and bought of EDWARD LEWIS scituate in Farnham Parish in the said County near TOTASKEY CREEK to her and her heirs and assignes for ever to be at her choice and election when she attaines to the age of twenty one years or Day of Mariage wch shall first happen

Item. I give and devise my Plantation land & housing whereon I now live; And ye Plantation (in case my Daughter make choice of the Twenty thousand pounds of Tob: as aforesd. which I bought of EDWARD LEWIS) unto my Sonn, LEROY GEORG; And my said Wife to be held by them during her naturall life and after her decease to the heires of the body lawfully to be begotten of my Sonn and for want of such issue to my sd Daugh-ter, MARGARET, and the heires of her body to be lawfully begotten; And for want of such issue to the heires & assignes of my said Wife, ELIZABETH, for ever; And my true intent and meaning is that in case my said Son dye leaveing issue of his body before my said Wife, then she to have no benefitt by right of Survivourship but that part and portion in the said land and premises to decend on such issue my said Sonn as might belong unto him liveing

Item All the rest & residue of my said Estate be it in ready mony, goods, cattle, servants horses, mares or other cattle I give and bequeath unto my said Wife and Sonn equally to be devided between them part and portion alike but my minde and will is that my Wife shall and may enjoy the male Cattle belonging to my Son benifitt of servants for the better maintenance & bringing up of my said Children untill my sd Son attain the age of Seaventeen years att wch time I doe hereby appoint that what is hereby granted to him be as his own dispose and to be invested therein as in Case he had obtained the full age of twenty one yeares And to prvent an unjust

THO: GEORG

appprisemt. that comonly viperously eats out the sides of Orphants Estate, my request is that my trusty and welbeloved Friends, Mr. EDWIN CONWAY, Mr. ARTHUR SPICER and JNO. TAVERNER take on them the Charitable oversight of this my Will and be aiding and assisting in the execution thereof unto my Executors And that they would inventory my personall Estate and to the best of their Judgmts. devid the same in specificall goods and chattles as they shall then be And to take a pticular accot. of what shall fall to my Sonns part (the goods & chatles being delivered to my Wifes custody again) And the same Accot. being Signed Receipt wayes to putt upon Record, But if my Wife remarry then such Husband to give security for my Sonns part to be delivered him as aforesaid

Item I give & bequeath unto my sd three Friends Twenty Shill. a piece to buy them Rings to wear in remembrance of me and twenty Shillings more to each of the Wifes of the sd Mr. EDWIN CONWAY & JOHN TAVERNER for the same purpose, And I doe hereby constitute and appoint my loving Wife and Son Execrs. of this my last Will and Testamt. provided and upon this condition the Bequest and devize of my land made unto my Wife joyning her in Joynt Tenancy with my said Sonn aforesaid be in Leiw and full satis-fction of her right of Dower of all and singuar my Estate real and personall And that she seale a release thereunto if occasion be or require; And I doe hereby make void and revoak all former Wills by me Wrote or spoake In Witness whereof to this my Will consisting with this of two Sheets of paper I have affixed my Seale att the Topp & sub-scribed to each sheet my name the day in the first sheet first above written

Signed Sealed delivered and by the sd

Testatr. published as his last Will & Testamt.   THO: GEORGE
     DENIS CARTY,   83
     PHILLIP HANINGS, JN: TAVERNER

Mr. JNO. TAVERNER & Mr. DENIS CARTY doth depose and say that they did see the Testatr. signe seale & publish this above mentioned Will as his last Will & Testamt. And that he was then in perfect sence at the signing & sealing thereof and further saith not

                                   JO: TAVERNER
                                   DENNIS CARTY

Probatr p Sacrament in Cur Com Rappa uno die 9bris 1683 et Recordatr xx6 die

pp.   AN INVENTORY and Apprismt. of the Estate of ROBERT KING by order of the
19-   Worshipfull Court by us the Subscribers October 10th 1683
20   To two 3 year old Steers; To one old Cow & one Steer yearling; To one old Gun;
      To 2 old Cattaile beds; 2 plaine rugs, 1 blankett, one old Shagg rug; To 2 pr old drawers, one wastecoate, To one pr wool cards, To 2 pr old yarn hose, To 2 old Chests; To parcell of old pewter, To one old drawing knife; To 2 old knives; To 3 old pailes; To one butter Tubb; To 2 old milk trays; To one old milk boule; To one old Bible; To 2 old baggs, To parcell of old lumber; one old frying pan; To two old weeding hoes, 1 old grubing hoe, one Childs standing Stoole; To one old Smoothing Iron; To 2 old Reaphooks
                                   Total   2821

WM. /\ MOSS
JAMES X KINGE
GEORG TAYLOR

Sworne to before me the day above written
                              p me   GEORG TAYLOR
Recordalr xx6 die 9bris Ano 1683

pp. IN THE NAME OF GOD Amen, I ELIZABETH CRASK of County of Rappae being sick
20- and weak of body yet of perfect sence and memory doe make this my last Will
22   and Testament in manner and form as followeth.

Imprimis I bequeath my Soule to God who gave it and my body to the dust from
whence it was taken to be decently interred with Christian burial at the discreation of
my Exector hereafter named in hopes of a joyfull resurection at the last day through
Jesus Christ or: Saviour

Item. I give and bequeath unto FRANCES MOSS, Daughter of my former Husband, THO-
MAS MOSS, one Negro woman called Flora, and the first and second child that the said
Negro woman shall bear I bequeath unto ELIZABETH MOSS, Daughter to my former hus-
band, THOMAS MOSS

Item. I will that FRANCES MOSS have the third child that the said Negro woman shall
bear and all that she shall bear to the said FRANCES and her heires for ever

Item. I will that the two Children that the said Negro woman shall happen to beare to
the use of ELIZABETH MOSS be and remain with the Mother untill they shall be one
yeare old And that then they may be taken away by the said ELIZA. MOSS

Item. I give to ELIZABETH one hoop a gold ring and I give unto FRANCES MOSS my
hoop & gold Ring that I weare on my hand

Item. I give unto ELIZABETH MOSS and FRANCES MOSS all my cloaths and apparrell that
I leave to be equally devided between them both

Item. I give to my God Daughter, ELIZA. MOSS, Daughter to WILLIAM MOSS, one Silver
box and one gold Ring with a Stone in it

Item. I give unto GEORGE MURRALL one two year old heifer

Item. I give unto my Sister, REBECCA MOSS, one Gown

Item. I give to ELLINR., Daughter of RICHARD STOAKES, one ten year old heiffer

Item. I give my Chest of Drawers to the abovesaid FRANCES MOSS

Item. I give the said ELIZABETH MOSS, Daughter of THOMAS MOSS, one feather bed
boulster red rug and one paire of chests

Item. To the above said FRANCES MOSS, I give one Sack, Cup of Silver & one small Silver
bodkin

Item I give unto ELIZABETH MOSS one Silver spoon and Siler bodkin

Item. I give unto ROBERT PARKER, Son of THOMAS PARKER, one heiffer of two yeares
old and in case of the death of the said ROBERT the heiffer is to be bestowed on any
other of the Sonns of the said THOMAS PARKER as he shall think sitt

And of my Estate that remaines when my legacies are satisfied I will that my debts be
fully paid & satisfied

Item. I appoint and ordaine THOMAS HERBERT of the Parish of Sittingborn and ELIZA-
BETH MOSS, Daughter of my former Husband, THOMAS MOSS, Execr. & Executrix joyntly
of this my last Will and Testament revoakeing all former Wills by me had and made &
doe declare this and non other to be my last Will and Testament moreover

Item. I will that when all my debts and Legacies are fully paid & satisfied that what of
my Estate doth remaine be equally devided between my Execr. & Execrx. and FRAN. MOSS

Item. I will that my Execr. & Execrx. do call THOMAS NEW to accompt for all the con-

cerns of my Husbands, Capt. EDMUND CRASK, or of mine that all hath been or shall be in
the hands of the said THOMAS NEW or in his Management alsoe I will that out of my
hoggs there be paid to FRANCES MOSS six Sowes one boar and three barrows

Item. I give unto my Brother, ROBERT MOSS, one Boar barrow of two years and a halfe
old And one other barrow of that age and one simple rugg

Item. I give unto REBECCA STOAKES, Wife of RICHARD STOAKES, my pallmata Hat And
one whole suite of Lynen throughout Shift and all

Item I give unto ELIZABETH NEWTIN, Wife of HENRY NEWTON, two pewter dishes, two
plates and one dutch Iron pott

Item. I give unto my God Child, ANN, Daughter of ALEXANDER ROBINS, one Silver
whistele with bells and currell

Item. I give unto FRANCES MOSS my Feather bed with red curtains and Vallence, red
rugg and boulster, two pillows and one paire of sheets

Item. I give unto ELIZABETH MOSS one blankett & two pillows

Item. I will that all my table linen be equally devided between the two Sisters, ELIZA-
BETH and FRANCES MOSS.

Item. I give unto THOMAS HERBERT my great Chest

Item. I give unto JOHN CRASK, a mourning Ring what were his Fathers and one pr of
Silver Buckles

Item. I give unto ELLEN CRASK two pairs of my shoes and one pair of Stopps

Item. I give my little Table in my Room to REBECCA STOAKES above mentioned and one
pewter dish, one pewter plate & two saucers & one spitt

Item. I give unto THOMAS HERBERT one heiffer bigg with calfe of three years old
called Maydere

Item. I give unto MARTHA, the Daughter of ABRAHAM STEPP, one heiffer of two years
old

Item. I give unto THOMAS PARKER SENR. two Dowils shirts

Item. I will that THOS. HERBERT have to his own use and behoofe my Negro woman,
Flora, for to serve him one yeare And that he also have my servant boy to make one
crop of his own pticular use and service, And what time the said Servt. boy hath longer
to serve I will that he serve it to ELIZABETH MOSS; And what now remaines of my pewter I give between the two Sisters, ELIZABETH and FRANCES MOSS.

Finally, I will that I be interred with my Husbands, and that my burying place be
enclosed with a decent pale.

In Consideration of all and singular these above recited premises and articles and
Testimony that this is my last Will and Testament I hereunto subscribe with my hand
and affix my Seale this 18th day of November in the yeare of or: Lord 1683

Item. I give unto my Brother, WILLIAM MOSS, one Silver seale
Signes Sealed and published
in prsence of us HENRY TANDEY,
          THO: PARKER, HENRY NEWTON   ELISABETH O CRASK

We the Subscribers doe by these prsents depose and say that we did see the within
named Testatrx. Signe Seale and publish this within written Will to be her last Will and
Testament and that she was then in perfect sence and memory at the signing and
sealing hereof As Witness our hands this 3 day of Janry. 1683/4
                                        HENRY TANDEY
                                        HENRY O NEWTON

Jurate sunt TANDEY et NEWTON in Cur Court Rappa Ano 1683/4
Test WM: COLSTON Cl. Cur
Probatr p Sacrament et Recordatr xx3 die

p.   IN THE NAME OF GOD Amen I PETER JOHNSON being very sick and weak in body
22   but in perfect sence and memory blessed be God doe make my last Will and
      Testament in maner and form as followeth

First, I bequeath my Soule to God that gave it and my body to be decently buried at the discreation of my surviving friends hopeing for a joyful Resurrection of the same by ye merrits of Jesus Christ and as for my worldly goods I dispose of them as followeth:

First my will is that my Son in Law, JNO. MARTIN, goe free and be for himselfe and that he have the Tuition of my Son, PETER JOHNSON, untill he be twenty yeares of age alwaies provided that the said JNO. MARTIN give my Son convenient Education & Maintenance & take no ill courses wherein if he faulters in any respect my will is that my Exectr, JAMES JACKSON, to take my Son, PETER, into his Guardianship and that he remaine with my said Executor the terme aforesaid. I give all my Estate to my Son, PETER JOHNSON, to remaine in the Custody of he that keepes my Child, care being taken to pay my Debts.

Lastly, I doe constitute my well beloved friend, JAMES JACKSON, to be my Executor of this my last Will and Testamt. revoaking all other wills heretofore made as Witness my hand & seale this 4 day of December 1682

Witness JAMES HARRISON,   PETER { } JOHNSON
        SUSAN ? H HAMMOND

Wee the above named JAMES HARRISON & SUSAN HAMOND doth depose and say that we did see the Testator signe seale and publish the above mentioned as his last Will and Testament and that he was then in perfect sence and memory, And further saith not

                                      JAMES HARRISON
                                      SUSAN ? H HAMOND

Jurati sunt HARRISON et HAMMOND in Cur Com Rappa 2d die Janry 1683/4

pp.   The Deposition of THOMAS SEARL aged 50 years or there abouts sworne saith
22-   that yor: depont. came to the house of JNO. LANKHORN to demand some tobacco
23   of Mr. WILLIAM WHEELER which was owing to yor: depont. from the said

WHEELER who then lay very Sick at the said LINKHORNs of wch. Sickness he the said WHEELER some small time after dyed, And at that time when yor: depont. was with him demanding his Debt, the said WHEELER declared that he had ordered JOHN LINKHORN to pay the said tobacco to ye depont. (if he then died) on wch. answer ye depont. was well satisfied and took leave of the said WHEELER and going to depart the Roome, Mr. WHEELER calld. to yor: depont. saying that if he died, JOHN LINKHORNE shold certainly pay me for that his full purpose and desyne was to give all his Estate to the said JOHN LINKHORNE who was to pay all his Debts after his decease, And the over plus wch. remained thereof he freely gave to the said LUCKHORNE; Further yor: depont. says that at the same time to the best of yor: deponts. knowledg and Judgmt. the said WM. WHEELER was in perfect sence mind and of a good disposing memory and further saith not

Sworn the 28th xber 1683 before me   THO: TT SEARLE
      LEROY GRIFFIN ss

The Deposition of ABRAHAM BUSH aged 61 yeares or thereabouts Sworn saith that yor: depont. was wth. Mr. WM. WHEELER when he lay sick at the house of JNO. LINCKHORN to demand a Debt due from said WHEELER to yor: depont., And that then he the said Mr. WHEELER declared to me that JNO. LINCKHORN should pay yor: depont., that was my due for that if he should dye his full resolves was that the said LINCKHORN should have all his Estate to pay his debts after his decease At wch. time the said WHEELER was to the best of yor: depont. Judgmt. in perfect sence & memory And further saith not

ABRAHAM BUSH ⊗

Sworne before me ye 28th xber 1683

LEROY GRIFFIN

Probatr p Sacrament Com et Recordatr ××4 die Januarii ano 1683/4

p. 23   Here is some part of a turning lave, one maindrill, fouwer turning tools, 2 old plaines, one smoothing filame, one old Joynter, one plow & 2 Irons, 14 moulding plaines & 2 augers & one pincer, 3 mortis Chissells & 2 peices of plank wch JNO. PAYNE & JOHN SANDERS according to their Judgments have apprized them at Three hundred Seventie pounds of tob:

JOHN PAYNE
JOHN SANDERS

Sworn to by JOHN SANDERS in the County Court of Rappae: 2 die Janry. 1683/4 et Recordatr.

pp. 23- 24   IN THE NAME OF GOD Amen. I JOHN MOTLIN of the Parish of Sittingbourne in the County of Rappa. being sick and weake in body but of sound and perfect memory make and ordaine this my last Will and Testament in manr. and forme following hereby revoaking all formr. Wills by me made And this to be my last Will and Testament

Imprs. I give and bequeath my Soule into the hands of Almighty God hopeing and trusting by the merritts of Jesus my Saviour to obtaine full and perfect remission of all my sins, And as for my body to the earth from whence it came to be buried in decent manner by my Executors hereafter named and as for my worldly Estate God hath been pleas'd to bestow upon me I bequeath as followeth:

3. I give and bequeath unto my two Sonnes, WILLIAM MOTLIN and HENRY MOTLIN, all that tract of land I am possessed of to be equally devided between them when they come of age, the said WILLIAM to have his first choice.

4. my will is that the rest of my per-sonall estate be equally devided between my three Sonnes, WM. MOTLIN, HENRY and JNO. MOTLEN.

I give & bequeath unto ELIZABETH RICHARDSON, one black heifer wch came of the called Blak Eyes to her and her heires for ever

5. My will is that my pesonall Estate be Inventoryed by DAVID STERNE & JAMES TRENT and according to quantity and quality to be deliver'd by my Executors hereafter named into my

6 three Sonns when they shall come to the age of one & twenty years.

My Will is that if either of my Sonns die without issue of their body lawfully begotten that then the Reale and personall estate return unto the next Survivor; And in case that all three decease before they come of age that then one third tract be deliver'd unto my Son in Law, JNO. SPICER, and the rest of my Estate to my Executors hereafter named.

I give unto KNIGHT RICHARDSON my 8. sarge Suite to be delivered to him prsently after my decease

My will is that DAVID STERNE have the care of my two Sonns, HENRY MOTLIN and JNO. MOTLIN and their parts of the Estate and to deliver it in kind to them when they come to the age of twenty yeares and as for my Son, WILLIAM, my will is that he choose one of my Executors to be his 9. Guardian wch he please

My will is that DAVID STERNE and JAMES TRENT being full and reale Executors to see this my last Will and Testament pformed

Itm. I give to RICHARD MATHEWS my Ozenbridge Suite. I give and bequeath unto Mr.

ARTHUR SPICER my Seale Ring. I give unto NATHANIELL ALEN one gold Ring. I give
unto ALICE TRENT one gold Ring. I give unto ELIZAB. KNIGHT one gold Ring;
  My will is that KNIGHT RICHARDSON have house and ground for fouer years and clear
upon any of my land except the Island & Calf Pasture.
  In Witness whereof I have hereunto sett my hand and seale this 7th day of Febry.
1683/4
  Sealed and Deliver'd in the presence of
          NATHANIELL ALLEN,
          KNIGHT K RICHARDSON,   JOHN ⴲ MOTLIN
          MARTIN ⑥ MIDDLETON
  Wee the undr. written doe depose and say that they did see the within named Signe
Seale and publish this within mentioned Will to be the last Will and Testament of the
said Testator, And that he was then in perfect sence and memory. As Witness or: hands
this 5th of March 1683/4
                                           KNIGHT ⴌ RICHARDSON
                                           JAMES ⴲ TRENT
    Jurati sunt RICHARDSON et TRENT in Cur Com Rappa 5 die Martii Ano 1683/4

p.   IN THE NAME OF GOD Amen I ELIZABETH HENLEY, now Wife of ROBERT HENLY,
24   and formerly Relict of JNO. ENGLISH deced being sick in body but in perfect
          mind and memory do make this my last Will and Testament as followeth.
  Imprs. I bequeath my Soule to God who gave it hoping in Jesus Christ my only Saviour
and Redeemer for Eternall Salvation and my body to the Earth from whence it was
taken with Convenient Christian buriall
  Secondly, I doe make my Husband, ROBERT HENLEY, my heire And I doe give all my
land that my former Husband, JNO. ENGLISH, gave me in his Will wch. before the pub-
lication of Matrimony to my last Husband I made over to my selfe by Deed indented and
recorded in the County Court of Rappahannock, And I doe now freely give it to him for
Ever
  In Witness whereof I have hereunto sett my hand and Seale this 2d of Aprill 1682
Signed & Sealed in the presence of us
          ALEXANDR. X DUDLEY   ELIZABETH ∧ HENLY
                WILLIAM BARBER
  ALEXANDR. DUDLEY was so sworn in Court 7th May 1684 to ye proffe of this before
recorded Will. ALEXR. DUDLEY the Subscriber did see ELIZABETH HENDLEY signe seale &
publish this to be her last Will and Testamt.
                                           WILL. BARBER
    Juratus est BARBER in Cur Com Rappa 6th die Martii 1683/4 et recordatr xr9 die

p.   AN INVENTORY of all and singular the Goods chattells and Debts belonging to the
25   Estate of Mr. THOMAS GEORG deceased taken and apprised by us whose names are
          hereunto subscribed and prsented to or: veiw by Mr. ELIZABETH GEORG his Relict
Executrix the 23d day of Febry. Anno Dom 1683/4 and is as followeth (Vizt.)
  Imprs. Nine cows young and old, Six steers young and old, a small Bull; fower young
cattle 2 yeare old, seaven yearling cattle, two feather bedds, bedsteads and other furniture to them as standing, a Flock bed truckle bedsted & other furniture, Ten leather
chaires, 4 wooden chaires, three tables and a forme with two joynt stooles & a desk, one
large Chest, 2 small ones, a box and small Dutch case.
  In the Milk House, a Chest, some casks and other lumber, three potts, Iron ladle and
iron driping pan and an iron grid iron

In the Kitchin: an iron fyre shovell & Tonges and 2 spitts & an iron flesh forke, a larg brass kettle, a small one and a brass skillet, ye kettle is defectv.

The horse called Swan. The horse toby. A miserable poor and old horse wch we cannot vallue above 0600. 80 lb. pewter at 8 pr. 2 roasting tubbs trays & some wooden lumber in the Kitchin

LINEN. One dozen diaper napkins, one dozen of Ozenbridge hapkins, one pr. Cours holland sheets, two table cloaths, one of ozenbridge ye other diaper; 2 course towells and one of diaper; 2 dowils, Mr. GEORGE;s wareing apparrell; a parcell of Bookes.

Servants. THO: BOLSTON 2 yeares 10 months to serve. JNO. HAWKINS neare 4 months to serve. SAML. EVANS about 11 months to serve. SUSAN ROBINSON by Custom about 10 months to serve

The present crop of Tob: a copper pott, a looking glass & 2 brass candletsticks

By a list of Debts good and bad togeather amounting to 38572

Item a Cart and wheels wth horse harness very old

> WILL BARBER
> DENNIS CARTY
> JOHN BAYLEY

The said ELIZABETH GEORG and the said Apprizers were all according to the intents of an Ordr. of Rappa Court sworne before me the day and yeare first within written

> LEROY GRIFFIN   83

Recordatr xx9 die Martii ano 1684

pp.   April Court 1684. IN THE NAME OF GOD Amen I JOHN WATSON of Sittingborn
26-   Parish in the County of Rappa: in Virginia, Planter, being very sick and weak
27   in body but of pfect memory & in mind praised be God therefore considering
      that it is appointed for all men once to dye and after Death to Judgment, doe
constitute and appoint this my last Will and Testament in maner and forme following
(that is to say)

Imprs. I give my soule into the hands of Almighty God my Creator hopeing by salva-tion only by the merritts of my Redeemer Jesus Christ whom I trust by his mighty power shall unite my body & soule being raised at the last day and to enjoy the blessed prsence of Almighty God to all Eternity, my body I ordr. to be buried decently at the discreation of my Executrix hereafter named And for my Estate both reale and personall and all such worldly goods cattles & chattells as it hath pleased God to bestow upon me in this mortall life I give and bequeath them in manner and form following

Itm. I give and bequeath all the land I am possessed of unto my two Sons JNO. WATSON & THOMAS WATSON, Alsoe I ordr. that my two Sons shall live and abide with their Mother untill they shall come to the age of one and twenty yeares each of them. I alsoe do ordr. that my Wife shall have the priviledge of the Plantation whereon I live untill my Son, JNO. WATSON, shall come to age and fulfill the yeares of one & twenty as alsoe after my Son shall attaine the age of one & twenty yeares I do give my Wife, PRICILLIA WATSON, the one halfe of my land Orchard & Plantation wherein I now live and the benefitt thereof during her life, As alsoe I doe ordaine give and bequeath unto the Child wherewith my Wife now goeth with that if it shall please God it be a man child it shall be equally concerned in the land with my Sons, JNO. WATSON & THOMAS WATSON, As alsoe my will is that if either or any of my Sons shall dye without lawfull issue that then the Survivor or Survivors shall inherit; that if my sons shall dye all of them with-out lawfull issue that then my land shall be devided between my two Daughters, SUSAN WATSON & ELIZA. WATSON, by equall devision, Alsoe my will & Testament is that if my Children shall be any way abused that then it shall be at the discretion of my friends hereafter named to remove them untill they shall be of age to Chuse their guardian

Item. I give unto my well beloved Wife, PRISCILLA WATSON, a gray Mare with her increas as alsoe my black rideing horse as alsoe the old horse I give myu Wife to be for the use of the house

Item. I give and bequeath unto my Son, JNO. WATSON, a sorrell Mare with hir increase and a gray horse aboute fower yeares old

Item A black Mare colt about two yeares old with her increase unto my Son, THO: WATSON

Item. I give the bay Mare with a Spring Tayle with her increase I give to my Daughter SUSAN

Item. I give and bequeath the bay Mares foale if it be not otherwise disposed of I give with her increase to my Daughter, ELIZABETH

Item. I give and bequeath unto my well beloved Wife, PRISCILLA WATSON, I give and bequeath the bed wherein I ly togeather with the furniture

JOHN ✗ WATSON

Item. I give and bequeath unto my Son, JOHN WATSON, the bed and furniture that is in the Chamber

Item. I give unto my Daughter, SUSAN WATSON, the bed that is in the Out Room

Item. I order that the yellow Steere with hornes be killed and used for the use of house keeping according as my Wife shall appointe

Item. All the rest of my goods and cattell my Chattells horses mares or whatsoever else of Estate belongs to me I order to be equally devided between my welbeloved Wife, PRISCILLA WATSON, and my Children, JNO. WATSON, THOMAS WATSON, SUSAN WATSON and ELIZ. WATSON as alsoe the Child or Children wherewith my welbeloved Wife, PRISCILLA, is now with child

Item. I doe hereby constitute give & bequeath unto my loving Friend, HENRY GORMAN, my back Sword & belt

Lastly, I doe hereby constitute and appoint my welbeloved Wife, PRISCILLA WATSON & JNO. WATSON to be Executrix & Executor to this my last Will and Testament he entering upon the Executorship when he comes to the age of twenty one years, And I doe hereby appoint my trusty and welbeloved Friends, Capt. DANIELL GAINES, Mr. FRANCIS SLAUGHTER, Mr. JNO. CATLET and Mr. WILLM. UNDERWOOD as Overseers of my Will soe far as to see an equall devision made of my goods & chattels & other Estate according to my Will and Testament, As alsoe I do hereby impower them to look after my Children, And in case they shall think fitt, upon just Complaint, to remove them as they shall see fit according to their discreation

Item. I order and appointe my Daughters, SUSAN WATSON & ELIZABETH WATSON to abide with their Mother untill they are married or attaine to full age.

In Witness whereof that I doe declare this to be my last Will and Testament contayning two sheets of paper writ on the one side and so read togeather Revoaking all former Wills wtsoever As Witness my hand and seale this sixth day of February One thousand Six hundred and Eighty three

Signed Sealed & pronounced to be   by me affixed
 my last Will & Testament, in the prsence
of us DAVID HOOMES   JNO. ✗ WATSON
       SAMUELL HENSHAW. WILL. HEATHER

I WILLIAM HEATHER within mentioned aged about fourty years doe attest upon oath this within writen Will to be the last Will and Testament of the within mentioned JNO. WATSON, And hereunto have sett my hand this 2d of Aprill 1684
                                                     WILL HEATHER

I SAMLL. HENSHAW within mentioned aged about three & twenty yeares doe attest upon oath this within written Will to be the wthin mentioned JNO. WATSON And hereto have sett my hand this 2d of Aprill 1684

                                        SAMLL. HENSHAW

Probatr. p Sacrament Comm in Cur Com Rappa 2 die Aprillis 1684

pp.   IN THE NAME OF GOD Amen. I THOMAS PERKINS being perfect in minde &
27-   memory but weak and sick of body doe make this my last Will and Testament in
28   maner and form follo: (Vizt.) I give my Soule into the hands of God that gave it
        in sure and certaine confidence of the mercies of Jesus Christ in the pardon of
all my sins and the assurance of my Resurrection at the end of the World And my body I
yeild it to the Earth from whence it came to be decently and Christianly buried And as
for my worldly Estate it hath pleased God to lend me, I bestow and give in manner and
form

Imprs. I give and bequeath my wearing gould ring on my hand to THOMAS PARKER, I
give and bequeath my Ring (that is due to me from the Estate of WILLIAM SARGENT)
unto ELIZABETH BLOMFEILD. I give and bequeath unto all my God Children a hdd. of
Tobo. a peice. I give and bequeath all the remainder of my Estate (my just Debts being
first satisfied) unto Capt. SAML. BLOMFEILD whom I make and constitute my Executor of
this my last Will and Testament as witness my hand and seale this 18th Decembr. 1683
Signed Sealed and Deliverd.   Given under my hand & seale
in prsence of us MARTIN JOHNSON,   THOMAS PERKINS
        MARY M JOHNSON

The Deposition of MARTIN JOHNSON aged fourty eight years or thereabouts sworn &
Examined saith that yor: depont. did see Mr. THOMAS PERKINS seale and deliver and own
the within written Will to be his act and deed and that the said PERKINS was in his right
sence and memory at the delivering the same to the best of yor: deponts. Judgmt. And
further yor: depont. saith not

                                        MARTIN JOHNSON

The Deposition of MARY JOHNSON aged fifty years or thereabouts sworn & examined
saith that yor: depont. did see Mr. THOMAS PERKINS own the wthin written Will to be his
act & deed & last Will and Testament And that the said PERKINS was in his right sence &
memory at ye delivering of the same to the best of yor: deponts. Judgmt. And further
yor: depont. saith not

                                        MARY M JOHNSON

MARY JOHNSON was sworn to this deposition before me the first day of Aprill 1684 and
did own every part of the abovesaid Deposition. Given undr. my hand the day and yeare
abovesaid

                        p me   DANIELL GAINES

Probatr in Cur Com Rappa 2 die Aprillis ano 1684

p.   IN THE NAME OF GOD Amen. I RANDOLPH PETERS being in perfect sence &
28   memory blessed be God for the same, doe make and affirmate this my last Will
        and Testament in maner and form following.
Imprimis I give and bequeath my soul unto God hoping that in and through the merrits death & passion of my Lord and Saviour Jesus Christ I shall inherit life everlasting
And my body to its earth And as for my worldly goods with which it hath pleased God to
bless me I give and bequeath as follow:
Imprimis I give & bequeath unto MARGARETT CURTIS and her heirs forever One hundred fourty two acres of land lying upon BARBARRA GOLDMARSH.

Item. I give and bequeath unto the said MARGARET CURTIS, one Cow and two yearlings marked with two crops and two holes as alsoe my working tools.

Lastly, I make & constitute and ordain the daid MARGARET CURTIS my full and sole Executrix. In Witness whereof I have hereunto sett my hand and Seale this 18th day of Febry. in the yeare of or: Lord One thousand Six hundred eighty and three

Signed sealed & delivered in the presence of us

GEORGE COLELOUGH,   RANDOLPH R P PETERS
ANTHONY SMITH, ANN SMITH

Juratus est SMITH in Cur Com Rappa 2d die Aprillis ano 1684 et Recordatr x6 die
The Depostion of GEORGE COLELOUGH aged about 29 yeares or thereabouts is ready to depose when by lawfull form called that yor: deponent did write the within mention;d Will of RANDOLPH PETERS and doth further say that he being in perfect sence and memory did appoint and ordaine and publish this within written as his last Will and Testament bearing date the 18th Febry. 1683

GEORGE COLELOUGH

Probatr p Sacrament WM. COLSTON, Cl Cur.

pp.   IN THE NAME OF GOD Amen. I ALEXANDR. ROBINS of the County of Rappa. being
29-   sick and weak but of perfect sence and memory doe make this my last Will and
30   Testament as followeth.

Imprimis I bequeath my soule to God that gave it and my body to the Dust from whince it was taken in sure and certaine hope of resurrection to Eternall life through my Lord & Saviour Jesus Christ And doe dispose of my Temporall Estate in maner & form following

Item I give and bequeath Six hundred and fifty acres of land that I have lying in the County of Rappa. back in the woods on the South side of the River on the branches of GILSONs & HODGKINs CREEKs unto my Daughters, REBECCA, ELIZA., JUDITH and ANA (Vizt) unto my Eldest Daughter, REBECCA, two hundred acres; unto my Daughter, ELIZA-BETH one hundred and fifty acres; unto my Daughter, JUDITH, one hundred & fifty acres and unto my Daughter, ANN, one hundred & fifty wch makes the sume of 650; as by Pattent will appeare, and Farther I will that they have hold & enjoy the said land to them and their heires for ever, but in case of the death of all or either of my said Daughters without issue of their body lawfully born, then I will that the land by this my Will belonging to all or either of my said Daughters soe dying without issue shall be and redound to the proper use and behooff and by the tenure and vertue of this my Will unto my Son, ALEXANDR. ROBINS, and his heires for ever.

Item. I do give and bequeath unto my Son, ALEXANDR., my land that I bought of WILLIAM BERRY above on the North side of the River containing One hundred thirty three acres or thereabouts And I will that it be confirmed to him and his heires forever by the said WILL. BERRY

Item I bequeath all my Cattle that are at this time in my possession unto my Wife and Children to be equally devided betwixt them to each of them their proper part share and share alike

Item I give and bequeath unto my Daughter, REBECCA, two pewter dishes which were her Grandmothers

Item I will if in case WILLIAM BERRY make not a good title to my Sonn, that the bond be sued and land be bought for my Son with the received effects

Item. I give unto my Wife all my houshold stuff goods and chattels & all moveables with all utensills thereunto belonging

Item I give unto JNO. COOK my Wifes Son, all and singular my wearing apparrell and my Kane with a Silver head

Item. I give my great gold Ring and a sett of Silver buttons to my Son, ALEXANDR. and alsoe my best hat and Silver hat band

Item. I give to my Daughter, REBECCA, my Silver Seale. I give to my Daughter, ELIZA-BETH one gold Ring

Item I give to my Son, ALEXANDR., one pr Breeches buttons of Silver

Item I give unto JNO. COOK my Gun that I had of JAMES BLACK and to my Son, ALEXANDR. my left handed Gun

Item I will that my horse and my horse colt be sould to pay my debts.

Finally, I will that my Son be kept at School the charg to be defrayed by the increase of his Cattle. Finally, I make and ordaine my beloved Wife, JUDITH, and my Friend, THOMAS PARKER, Executrix & Execr. of this my last Will & Testament Revoaking and disanulling all former Wills by me had and made declaring this and non other to be my last will and Testamt. Witness my hand and Seale this 16th day of Febry 1683.
Signed sealed and published in

THOMAS PARKER,   ALEXANDR. ROBINS
SUSANA WILLIAMS

Wee the Subscribers doe hereby declare & depose that they did see the within written Testatr. signe seale and publish the within mentioned Will as his last Will and Testamt. and was then in perfect sence & memory to the best of or: knowledg and further saith not

THOS. PARKER
SUSAN O WILLIAMS

Probatr p Sacrament Recordatr x6 die Aprillis Ano 1684

p.   December the 4th 1683
30   IN THE NAME OF GOD Amen. I THOMAS HARPER of the County of Rappa. in the
        Parish of Farnham being very sick and weak but of perfect memory doe make and designe this my last Will and Testament. I doe bequeath my Soule unto the Lord that gave it me and my body to the grave decently to be buried in a Christian burial

Imprs. All my debts being honsestly satisfied & paid, that then it is my desire that my welbeloved Wife, MARY HARPER, and JNO. HARPER, my Eldest Son, be joyntly Executors of all my personall Estate moveable & Immoveable & further most is my desire that all my land be equally devided between my three Sons, JNO. HARPER, SALOMON HARPER and THOMAS HARPER than my desire is that my Wife and Eldest Son, JNO. HARPER, be possest with the aforesaid land until my two youngest sonnes doe come to age provided my Wife should marry any such pson who by his prodigallyty wast consume & destroy ye aforesaid land, then my Son, JNO. HARPER, to take it into his Custody until they come to age. Furthermore I doe bequeath unto my Son, JOHN HARPER, one Servant boy named WM. CASSANBOUGH and one Gunn.

In Witness hereof I have hereunto set my hand & seale
Sealed & acknowledged in the presence of us
Test   HENRY WATKINS,   THO: X HARPER
        JNO. BONNER, JOHN D STEWARD
Probatr p Sacrament HENRY WATKINS et JOH: STEWARD 2 die Aprillis 1684 in Cour Com Rappa et Recordatr x6 die

p.   AN INVENTORY of the Estate of THOMAS JOHNSON deced
30   To an old Case without Lyning; 2 old torn Shirts, 1 old torn west Coat; pr old
        leather drawers, 2 pr old Shoes; 1 old knife & old Tob: box; old pr. tonges, one

pistoll with the stock broke, To oneCut gun with a Fracture in the barrill soe low one
cannot reach it; one hhd. Tob:, one pcell   Total   440
    by Bill 1000 Tob. & Cask; To falling cuting up & maling 500 Railes; To funerall charges
and sheet for his funerall
Record 17 die Aprilis 1684

pp.   May Court Ano 1684
31-   IN THE NAME OF GOD Amen I ROBERT GULLOCK of County of Rappa being sick
32   and weak in body but of sound & perfect memory Thanks be to Almighty God for
        the same And knowing the uncertainty of this transitory life and that all flesh
must yeild unto Death when it shall please God to call, Doe make constitute and ordaine
this my last Will and Testament in manner & form following, Revoaking all other Wills
and Testaments by me heretofore made & declared either by word or writing and this to
be taken for my last Will and Testament and no other. I committ my soule to Almighty
God my Maker in sure and certain hope of a joyfull & glorious Resurrection at the last
day, And my body to the Ground from whence it came, And as for my temporall Estate
wherewith it hath pleased God to bless me withall I give and dispose as followeth
    I will and bequeath all my lands and tenements to be equally devided between my
Daughter, JANE GULLOCK, and the Child which my Wife is now priviment insent withall
whether boy or girle to them and their heires for ever
    My will is that all my Sheepe shall be kept upon the Plantation till my aforesaid
Daughter, JANE GULLOCK, and the Child which my Wife is now bigg with all attaine to
the age of one and twenty yeares or marry; And then to be equally devided between
them, Except one third part of the weathers which I give to my said Wife dureing her
life
    Item My will is that non of my hoggs shal be removed of the Plantation, but shall be
and remaine all for the good of the abovesaid Children, Except my Wife live upon the
Plantation then my will is that she shall have one third
    Item I will that two thirds of all my Cattle shall be and remaine for the good of the said
Children equally to be devided between them and the other third to my Wife
    Item I give unto the abovesaid Children all my linen plate and three feather bedds
with furniture curtains & vallence and doe leave the whole tuition of my Daughter,
JANE GULLOCK unto my Wife and Sister VAULX
    Item I give unto ROBERT PAYNE one young Sorrille horse branded with (JG
    Item I give unto ELIZABETH ROWZEE one young Mare about four yeares old wch said
Mare comonly useth bout JOHN WILLIAMS Plantation
    Item I give unto my Loveing Wife my horse Dick with side Sadle bridle halter and
whip
    Item my will is that all the rest of my horses & Mares except the two old Cart horses
shall be and remaine to my abovesaid Children to be equally devided between them at
one and twenty years of age or Marriage wch shall first happen, Also I request my
Cozen, EDWARD ROWZEE, that he should be carefull to look after everything bequeathed
to my two Children and to brand the Colts and mark the Sheepe and hoggs for their use,
And for his Care & paines I give him out of the said Stock every forth yeare a Mare or
horse Colt
    Item I give unto my loving Wife two feather bedds with furniture
    Item my will is that after Mr. DEANs Lease is expired for the Plantation he now lives, I
will and bequeath the use of it unto my loving Friend, ROBERT BROOKE, untill my
Daughter, JANE GULLOCK, shall attaine the age of one & twenty yeares makeing no wast
of the timber, but for the use of the Plantation & fencing And leave it tenantable and if

my Daughter, JANE, or other Child shall happen to die before they attaine the age of
one & twenty, then I will the said Plantation to the said ROBT. BROOKE and his heires for
ever not exceeding above 100 acres of land

    Item I give unto ROBT. BROOKE my old Horse, Puppey

    Item I give unto my Cozen, EDWARD ROWZEE, my old Horse Jack withall the harness

    Item all the rest of my Estate after my debts legacies & funerall expenses discharged I
give and bequeath unto Mr. JOHN FOXHALL and Mr. ROBERT VAULX, whom I make Executors of this my last Will and Testament Requesting them to pay all my lawfull Debts
whether by Bill Bond or Account with as little trouble in the Law as they can.

    In Testimony whereof I have hereunto put my hand & Seale Ithis 26th day of Febry
Anno Dom 1683

Signed Sealed & delivrd. in the
prsence of EDWARD ROWZEE   ROBT. ℞ GULLOCKE
        TOBIAS INGRAM, RO. BROOKE

    I desire this to be annexed as a Codicil to my last Will and Testament. Whereas I have
not already disposed of by my Will of my maide Servant, MARY, therefore I desire & will
is that my loveing Wife shall have her during the time she have to serve according to
assignement.

    Item it is my will & desire and I doe freely bequeath unto my loveing Friends, Mr. JOHN
FOXHALL, Mr. ROBT. VALX, Mrs. MARY VAULX, Mr. JOHN DEANE & Mrs. JANE DEANE, Mr.
WILLIAM CLAPHAM and Mrs. MARY CLAPHAM each of them a Gold ring of 10 S. price
after my decease

    TOBIAS INGRAM and EDWARD ROWZEE doe depose & say that they did see the within
named Testatr. signe seale and publish this within mentioned as his last Will and Testament And that he was then in perfect sence and memory to the best of their knowledge
                                         EDWARD ROWZEE
                                         TOBIAS INGRAM

    Jurati sunt ROWZEE et INGRAM in Cur Com Rappa 7 die May 1684

pp.   IN THE NAME OF GOD Amen. The last Will and Testament of EVAN MORGAN of the
32-   Freshes of Rappahannock River in Virginia, Planter, being in perfect sence &
33   memory but sick and weak in body, Maketh and ordainith this his last Will and
        Testament in form and manner following

    Imprs. I give and bequeath my soule into the hands of my Creator and Deare
Redeemer hopeing through his merritts to be saved at the last day

    Item I give and bequeath my body to the Earth from whence it came to be decently &
Christianly buried according to the discreation of my Executrix hereafter mentioned

    Item I doe give & bequeath unto my Godson, MAXFIELD BROWNE, my Wifes youngest
Son, two able men Servants sound in their limbs & well in health each of them having
five or six yeares to serve to be delivered my said Godson at the age of eighteen yeares
old in the roome and stead of my two men Servants wch. now I have (Vizt.) THOMAS
GANIONS and JOHN ROBINSON & I doe Ordr. and appointe that if in case my Wife, ELIZA-
BETH, doe alter her condition by marriage any time before the said Servants, THOMAS
and JOHN, be free that then my loving friend MALLACHY PEALE to take the said Servants into his care and custody for the good of my Godson. And alsoe my Godson if he
thinks fitt soe to doe

    Item I doe give and bequeath unto my said Godson one hundred & twenty acres of land
being of a tract of land of two hundred & twenty acres which JOHN ROSE is now liveing
& seated upon to him and his heires for ever

    Item I doe give and bequeath unto my said Godson, two good Cawses of the age of five

or six years old being with Calfe or Calfes by their sides to be delivered to him at the age
of eighteen yeares. I doe give and bequeath unto my said Godson one feathr. bed and
bowlster with a good Rugg & a paire of Blanketts suitable thereto to be delivered at the
age aforesaid.

I doe give and bequeath unto my Wifes youngest Daughter, ELIZABETH BROWN, two
good cowes with calfes or Calfes by their sides of the age of five or six yeares old and
alsoe one good feather bed and bowlster with Rugg and blanketts suitable, to be delivered her at the age of eighteen years or day of marriage and alsoe one young Mare of
one or two yeares old to be delivered as aforesaid

Item I doe give and bequeath unto my Wifes Sonn, JOHN BROWN, one good Cow wth.
Calfe to be deliverd. him at the age of twenty one yeares old

Item I doe give and bequeath unto my Wifes Sonn, WILLIAM BROWN, one good Cow
with Calfe by her side to be delivered when he keeps house and all my Carpenter tooles

Item I doe give and bequeath unto my boy, THOMAS BOOTH, the time he hath to serve
me by Indenture or other wayes And give him one hhd. of Tob: to pay his passage to
England, Always provided he returns there, but if not that he serve his time with my
Friend, MALLACHY PEALE, he paying my Wife twelve hundred pounds of Tob:

Item (after my Debts are paid) I doe give and bequeath unto my loveing Wife, ELIZA-
BETH, & unto my loveing Friend, MALLACHY PEALE, all the rest of my Estate both reale
and personall; And doe nominate and ordaine them joynt Executor and Executrix of this
my last Will and Testament.

In Witness of these presents I have hereunto sett my hand & Seale this twenty fourth
day of August One thousand six hundred Eighty three Ano. 1683
Signed Sealed & deliverd. in prsence of us
    JOSIAH MASON,   EVAN A MORGAN
    THOMAS T JONES
    THOMAS BOOTH

JOSIAH MASON doe depose & say that he did see the within Testator signe seale and
publish this within and abovewritten to be his last Will and Testament and that he was
then in perfect sence and memory
                                     JOSIAH MASON

Probatr p Sacrament Comm
The Deposition of THOMAS JONES aged thirty three yeares or thereabouts saith that he
was prsent when EVAN MORGAN of this County of St. Marys Parish made his last Will
and Testament and was a witness thereunto And likewise doe further aver and declare
that he saw the said MORGAN Signe & Seale the same, Acknowledging it to be his last
Will & Testament And delivered the same to Mr. MALLACHY PEALE but what was thereon
inserted he is ignorant and further saith not
                         THOMAS T JONES

Sworn before me this 5th day of May Anno Dom 1684
                         ANTHONY SAVAGE

Recordatr xx5 die Maii anno 1684

pp.   IN THE NAME OF GOD Amen, this the twelvth day of March in the yeare of or:
34- Lord God 1682/3, I SAMUELL FLOYD being sick in body but of good and perfect
35   memory praised be God doe constitute & ordaine this my last Will and Testament
     in maner and forme following
Imprs. I bequeath my soule unto Almighty God my heavenly Maker in full hopes of
Remission of all my sins and my body to the Ground to be burried in Christian burriall,
And as for my worldly goods whereof it hath pleased God to bless me withall, I give and

bequeath them all whatsoever as well what is in my own Custody as what is in the Custody of any other person whatsoever, As all Debts which are by any meanes owing unto me whether by Bill or other waies, And all dues in Generall unto ANDREW BOYER his heires and assignes for Ever, And I doe hereby make the said ANDREW BOYER sole Executor of this my last Will and Testament as Witness my hand the day and yeare abovesaid

Testes Signd. BRIDGITT ⅝ SOUTHWELL,   SAMUELL ⅅ FLOYD
        JOHN BEATSON

The Deposition of JOHN BEATSON aged 39 yeares or thereabouts saith that whereas SAMUELL FLOYD lately deceased the last yeare now past before the date hereof was Resident in the house of one FRANCIS TAYLOR, And there being in an exceeding weak condition by reason of a sore legg which pleased Almighty God to (blurred) which (blurred) that he was not able to help himself, was brought by the said TAYLOR to the house of ANDREW BOYER And imediately after his coming thither, the said ANDREW BOYER demanded of him where his Chest was and what Toba: he had due unto him, Whereupon the said SAM. FLOYD told him of severall parcels of Tob: which was due unto him as alsoe of some which was due unto him for worke, And the said ANDREW BOYER did owe at that time unto the said FLOYD two Barrells of Corne for work, And likewise the said FLOYD told the said ANDREW BOYER of two Bills wch. had for Tob: due unto him (Vizt.) JOSHUA LAWSON Bill and DANLL. JACKSONs Bill, the wch. Bills the said BOYER without delay gott into his Custody, and further the said FLOYD told him that his Chest was at the house of the said FRANCIS TAYLOR aforesaid And the said TAYLOR did owe unto him severall goods expressing what goods they were which he had lent unto him, And the said TAYLOR had promied to pay ye like goods in kind the next year following, And Alsoe the said FLOYD told him that CHARLES SNEAD did owe him a considerable quantity of Toba: but yor: depont. cannot prossitively declare the just sum but according to the best of his remembrance it was well towards (if not altogether) a thousand pounds of Tob: Whereupon yor: Depont. being then a Servant to the said BOYER was commanded by his said Master to write a Will and thereby to bequeath unto him the sd BOYER all and whatsoever the said FLOYD was possest with, As alsoe whatsoever was due unto him by any meanes whatsoever. The which when yor: depont. had writt he read to the sd FLOYD and the said BOYER comanded him to Assigne it, But the said FLOYD refused to doe the same saying he did not know what it was, Whereupon the said BOYER fell into a Passion, And did inhumanly revile the said FLOYD with many approbrious and ignominious words and divers threats saying that if he would not Assigne it, he would turn him out doores, And therefore (as yor: depont. doth imagine) more out of scare than Love he did assigne the same; And Thereupon without delay the said BOYER sent yor: depont. to the aforesaid TAYLORs to fetch his Chest, but the said TAYLOR would not deliver the Chest to yor: Depont. saying it was not paid for; But gave yor: depont. Lycence to take what was in it and it was full of Cloaths and very good goods the which yor: depont. brought back to his Masters. Now Imediately after this the said ANDREW BOYER himselfe went to the said TAYLORs house and at his returne from thence he shewed yor: depont. a Bill wch. the said TAYLOR had assigned unto him for the payment of the goods aforesaid, & alsoe the said TAYLOR had obleidged himself to bring the Chest to the house of the said BOYER and according to the best of yor: deponts. remembrance he had likewise a Bill of Mr. CHARLES SNEAD for the Toba: aforesaid, And finally the said FLOYD lay in a sad and deplorable condition in the hogg house of the said BOYER, And when it was any quantity of Rain the water run under him And there he remained in this lamentable & disconsolate condition when yor: depont. was free from the said BOYER wch. was 7th day of October last past, And further yor: depont. saith not.

                                        JOHN BEATSON

Maii 7th 1684
JOHN BEATSON maketh oath in open Coaurt to the truth hereof
Test WM. COLSTON, Cl Cur Com Rappa
Recordatr xx4 die Maii Anno 1684

p.   Aprill the 4th 1684
35   The Inventory of ELIAS ROBERTS Estate To one wool bed and covering; To one
            pott; To a parcell of Nayles   Total 350 Tob:
Recordatr Test WM. COLSTON Cl Cur

p.   AN APPRAISEMENT of the Estate of PETER JOHNSON deceased as it was apprized
36   by JAMES ORCHARD and FRAS. TAYLOR upon Oath on the 14th day of Janry.
            1683/4 by vertue of an Ordr. of Court
One Cow and yearling; One heiffer, one two year old Bull, ten sows and hoggs; 3 barrells 4 bushells of Indian Corne at 130 lb Tob: p barrall; one bushell beanes, one iron
pott & hookes, 3 wedges, one narrow axe, one spitt, one unfixt gun, one Chest, one tray
of salt, Due from SUSAN HAMOND - (100) 53 lb. Bacon at 4 lb pr., a parcell of other meate,
one bagg, 2 hhd. carried of ye Plantacon by Mr. GEORG JONES, 4 parcells Tob: hanging
Apprised by us   JAM: ORCHARD
                                                        FFRA: FT TAYLOR
     May the 7th 1684. JAMES ORCHARD sworne in open Court that he made a true apprise-
ment of the Estate of PETER JOHNSON deced that was exhibited to him. JAMES JACKSON
did then make Oath that he did Exhibitt the whole Estate of the said PETER JOHNSON to
the sd Appraisers
     Recordatr xx4 die Mail Ano 1684

p.   THE APPRISMENT of Left in the hands of RICHARD HOBBS deced by JOHN
36   COMPTON
            3 pr mens yarn stockins, 3 pr Irish stockins; one pr ticking beddes; parcell
worsted lace, black thread & a pcell Silk; 1 pr Childrens hose, 3 ells flaxen cloath, 2 yds
white Callico, 7 yds fine searge, 2 thousand pins, Goods not in Mr. HOBBS inventory, one
pr mens shoes, one doz. spoons, 5 yds Scotch cloath, 8 yds blew linen, 8 yds flannell, 3
yds of Norviwich stuff, one pr Childrens stockins; 11 yds white Callico   657
     Recordatr in Cur Rappa xx4 die Maii Ano 1684

pp.   IN THE NAME OF GOD Amen. I HENRY SMITH being sick and weake in body but in
36-   perfect memory doe make this my last Will and Testament in maner & form
37   following: I give & bequeath my soule to Almighty God who gave it me in full
            hope of Salvation in and through the merritts of my Blessed Saviour Jesus Christ
I give and bequeath my body to the Earth from whence it came to be Christianly buried
by the discreation of my friends
     Item I give & bequeath my worldly goods in manner and form following my debts
first paid
     Item I give and bequeath to my Sonn, TOBY SMITH & HENRY SMITH, my whole tract of
land I live on to be equally devided between them and their heires for ever, but if in
case there be a valluable Seate of land cleard, in MATRUMS NECK and is justly found &
survayed, my Will is that my Son, HENRY SMITH, have it. And then he have only ye
land that is above the Creek called the GREAT CREEK, whereon GEORG now liveth to him
& his heires for Ever
     I give and bequeath to my beloved Wife one sorrell paceing horse with a side Sadle to
her and her heires for Ever

I give and bequeath all the rest of my goods & chattels to be equally devided between my Wife and two Sonns Share & Share alike

Item I bequeath my loveing Wife and EDWARD ADCOCK, Execrs: of this my Will and Testamt., for the pformance & managing hereof.

Item I bequeath Col. WM. LOYD & Mr. SAML. PEACHEY Overseers to see this Will pformed

Item I doe make null & void all other Wills by me at any time made or caused to be made As Witness my hand & seale this fifteenth day of Aprill 1684

Signed & Sealed in prsents of

    GEORG COLCLOUGH,   HEN: SMITH

    ROGER WATERS, JOHN WEBB

Wee the Subscribers doe depose and say that we did see the within named Testator signe seale & publish this within written to be his last Will and Testamt. and that he was then in perfect sence & memory at the signing sealing and publishing to the best of their knowledg

                                GEO: COLCLOUGH

                                JOHN WEBB

Proved by the Oaths of GEORGE COLCLOUGH and JOHN WEBB in the County Court of Rappa the 4th day of June 1684

pp.   AN INVENTORY of the Estate of THOMAS PERKINS Clerk apoprised the 15th of
37-   Aprill 1683/4
38   2 dear skins, 1 canonical gowne, 1 Cape Gown, 1 Dimity Coate, 1 old plush coate,
      1 old silk wast coate & Girdle, a parcell of old Cloaths, 2 dimity west coate &
crawers & 1 black britches, 5 yds Coulerd callico, 11 ells of Bengall, 3 shirts & pr drawers, his small waring linen, 1 pr new, 2 pr old Stockins, 1 steel box, knives, sisors & razors & tongs, lumber in the Drawers of the desk, pewter & tin buckells & 4 S. in mony, 3 old perriwiggs, one old hatt, 1 desk & seal skin case, 1 new black walnut chest, one old one, one Bible & Common Prayer Book, another parcell of books, some small things in the till of a chest; a broken sadle & spancills, one horse.

An Accot. of Bills & Debts. Col. NOELL, WM. MILLS, ROWLAND THORN, THOMAS FLEWELLING, PATRICK JACK, JOHN CHIRCHELL, NATHANIEL ALLEN, JOHN HOME, JAMES TOMPKINS

                  Apprised by us   ROBERT PLEY
                                          MARTIN JOHNSON

Sworn before me this 15th of Aprill 1684
                 DANIEL GAINES
Recordatr xx4 die Junii 1684

pp.   August Court Anno 1684
38-   AN INVENTORY of all and singular the Estate late of Major HENRY SMITH deced
39   taken and apprised in psuance of an Order of Rappa Court by us whose names are
      hereunto subscribed as ye same was prsented to veiw by _ ELIZABETH SMITH
ye Relict of ye said Major ye 12th day of June 1684 & is as followeth (Vizt.)

Seaven Cowes with Calves by their sides; five Cowes more; 4 Steers 2 of them about 5 yeares ye other about 3 yeares; 8 yearling cattle & one other not at ye prsent to be found; a Bull, 2 heifers, one lame Stone horse called Sampson, a horse given by Major SMITH in his Will to his Wife and comonly called Mr. SMITHs Riding Nagg; an old Mare (as we informed) of 19 years wth a yrling colt, a dark bay stone horse; 23 Ewe and 2 Ram sheep at 90 p sheep; 14 lambs at 45 p lamb;

In one of ye lodging Chambers above staires, a table and 2 leather Chaires. In ye same Chamber a standing bedsted wth curtains & vallence, a feather bed boulstr. & furnitr. as they now stand

In ye other room above staires an old half headed bedsted wth an old bed and such furniture. In ye same Room a Cradle, a spinning wheel, a pcel of wool & a standing stool for a Child.

In ye Hall, 3 old tables, a dozen of leather chaires, a deale Chest, a pr. of Iron dogges, a pr. of Iron tongs, a pr. of larg Stilliards, two sickles

In Mr. SMITHs Lodging Chamber, a feather bed wth furnitr. wth a standing bedsted wth curtaines & vallance, and old truckle bedsted, a very old bed therein wth such fur- nitre, a table and fourme wth fower low leather chaires, a Court Cubbard and 1 chest, all very old, a looking glass & a pcell of Earthen ware & a few old bookes, two old Rapiers and an old beld & scabbard; five silver spoones at 60; 1 of to p spoone two other small spoones & a silver dram cupp, a Case of six knives, very old table Cloaths, thirteen napkins & a cople of towells, two yards of haire shagg. THOMAS AINS Six months to serve, GERRARD FITZ GARRALL about 9 months to serve

In the Kitchin, unserviceable Still, a dozen of plates and two larg pewter dishes, a pewter flaggon, a nine pint pott; a pewter tankard and Salt, a little brass pestle and Mortar & an old brass kettle, an Iron kettle, 2 iron potts both old & small. 2 iron potts, 1 old broken Iron pestell, a small Iron frying pan, 2 pr pott racks, a ladle & fleshforks, 42 lb. of old pewter at 5 l of Tob: p L, and Old unfixed gunn two old Iron ffrowes, two old sadles & bridles, a Cart and a very old pr. of wheels, an old Boate, an old brass warming pann, a cross cut saw, 3 wedges, a Tob: cutting kniffe, an old pr. of Brass seales, a Gunn, a file and a latche, a stray horse cannot gett   Total   21010

                 THO: HARWAR
                 WILL. YOUNG   Apprisrs.
                 JOHN RICE
                 JO: TAVERNER

August 6th 1684 Me. That Mr. THO: HARWAR, Mr. WILL YOUNG & Mr. JNO. TAVERNER were this day sworn in Court

                        Test WM. COLSTON Cl Cur

Recordatr xxx die Augusti 1684

pp.   August 4th 1684
40-   AN INVENTORY and Apprisement of the Estate of Mr. ROBERT GULLOCK deceased
41   taken by Mr. ROBERT MOSS, Mr. ROBERT PLEY & THOMAS PARKER by order of
        Court

Imprs. To 8 cowes about 6 yeare old apeice, To 2 heiffers 3 yeares old apeice, 3 heiffers 2 yeare old, 3 Bulls at 3 year old, 4 yearlings & 4 calves, 1 Cow about 6 yeare old at Mrs. GIBSONs, 1 heiffer and a Bull about 2 yeare old apeice, a cow about 4 yeare old, 2 steers about 5 yeare old other about 3 yeare old, a cow about 4 yeare old & a bull bout 2 yeare old

Cattle at RICHD. FRENCHes, To one Cow tenn yeares old and a Calfe, 1 cow 5 yeares old and a Calfe, at Mr. CLAPHAMs, 1 cow and a Calfe, To one bay mare 8 yeares old & her colt named Buck. To one Mare at JAMES YATES 3 yeares old, To one mare 16 yeares old & her Colt; To 2 young geldings about 3 years old, To one mare about 7 yeares old, To 18 sheep young and old, To 1 case of pistolls and holsters and Simiter; To 1 other case of Pistolls screwed, 1 bed tick and boulster, 8 yards and 1/2 of bedtick; 1 sarg coate and breeches lined; 1 leather west Coate & breeches & one Buckskin, 1 riding Coate and one Coate and one Kerzy ditto; 2 felts, 2 pr old sheets and one old Coate, 8 old diapr. and Damask nap-

kins & diapr. Table cloath & a small parcell of old Linen napkins, 9 ounces of Silver, 2
pr of Stilliard, One check and a parcell of old Lumber in it; 7 lb. of Powder and a pcell of
Shott; 3 old chests, 1 great two small; 1 Feathr. bed and bedsted bowlsters & 2 pillows &
blanket all old, one othr. old Feathr. bed and bedstead wth their apptenances, To 1 old
bed in the Chimney Corner, 1 old Pillion & few old Shoemakrs. knives; To 6 old gunn
barrells, 2 pr of pott racks & an old gunn lock & pcell of old Iron & an old pr. of Bootes. a
parcell of old lumber in a Shed, a pcell of Carpentrs. and Coopers tooles, 4 saws & 2
sickles, To 2 old Bibles, a looking glass, an old sadle Trooprs. & one pr. andirons, an old
pestell and old grubbing thoe, 2 old axes, 3 Grind stones and a plow, 2 brass kettles, 2
brass Candlesticks, 1 spice morter and an old Skillett; To 3 gunns, a parcell of deal
boards & an old Cart; parcell of wooll, to 23 pr. shoes due from THO: SCUPS, 40 head of
hoggs runing in the woods, a list of Bills of Debts due to ye aforesd Estate.
  Imprs. One Bill of EDMUND CUNSTOCK alias INDIAN NED, one Bill of JAMES TOMPKINS,
one Bill of JOHN ROLTs, one Bill of THO: PARKERs for 1000 whereof there is 440 & en-
dorsed upon ye Bill there is still due 0573; against which he hath acct. 300 for teaching
ROBT. PAYS; one Bill of GEORGE BOYCEs, one Bill of FRAN: PEIRCE to be paid p Doctr.
HUBBART, one Bill of JAMES TOMKINS whereof nine hundred & fower is paid; one Bill of
NICHO. FRENCHes, one Bill of NICHO. FRENCHes for 2285 wehreof pd 450; one Bill of JOHN
AMOSE, one other Bill of JOHN AMOSE, By Bills 11073 whereof is paid 1744
  The sume of ye whole Estate Togeather wth Bill debts is 41560
  In Obedience to an Ordr. of Court bearing date May ye 7th 1684, we the Subscribers
have taken an Inventory & apprismt. of ye Estate of Mr. ROBERT GULLOCK, As Witness
or: hands August 4th 1684
Sworn before me this 4th of August 1684   ROBERT MOSS
      HEN: AWBREY   ROBERT PLEY
                                                       THO: PARKER

  Recordatr. xxx die Augusti 1684

pp.   AN INVENTORY and Apprisement of ye Estate of HENRY MUNCASTER by Ordr. of
41-   Rappa Court taken June ye 16th 1684
42   3 Cows with Calves, 1 Steer 3 yeares old, 1 yearling Bull, 1 sett Coopers tooles old
          with 3 wedges, 1 old Chest, pr. plaine shoes, pcell of old cloaths, 2 old books, 40 lb.
old Pewter, 2 Iron potts & one pr Pott racks tongs & Grid Iron; 1 parcell of old lumber, 2
old gunns, 1 smoothing Iron, paire bellows, one old Table and form, one old Couch and
Cutting knife, 2 old Cattalale bedds, 1 Rugg, 2 old Matchcoates, 1 old spade; 2 old hoes, 1
pestell & old sadle, 1 old Feather bed and rugg; 1 old Cow bell, parcell of hoggs
                                          Total 3705
Sworne before me the 16th day of   Apprised the day and yeare above written
June 1684   HEN: AWBREY   by us   ROBERT R PARKER
                                                      THOMAS / MUNDEY

  Recordatr xxx die Augusti Ano 1684

p.   AN INVENTORY and Apprisement of the Estate of ROBT. JONES of this County of
42   Rappa deceased as it was presented to us the subscribers by the Widdow May ye
        17th 1684
Imprs. one pr white blanketts, old red Coverlet, one little pillow, one small looking
glass, very good Couch, one old INDIAN Staff & 2 baskitts, one razor very old, one old
Comb, 3 old knives & old lock, parcell old axes and hoes, one other good axe, one little
brass kettle, old Rumlett, 2 glass bottles, pcell old lumber, a cask & sifter, three old
payles & an old buckett; one old hammer & peices, one washing tubb; 5 old trays small

butter pott & earthen pann, 6 small INDIAN panns, 3 old spoones, little wooden dish
platter and skimmer, one Canvas bagg, 5 Tob: hhds., pcell flax undrest, the stock of
Cattle belonging to ye Estate of ROBT. JONES amounted to 12175; three Cows the princi-
ple stock put in by me WILLIAM MOSS, And they to runn for the one halfe to the said
ROBERT JONES, the number, age & vallue; one cow & calfe, fower Steers 3 yeares old, one
Steer fower yeares old, two 2 yeare old Cattle, 3 yearlings Total 2880 the halfe 1440
   This is the true Accot. of ROBERT JONES Estate as it was prsented by the said Widdow
wch. was Inventories and apprised by us the Subscribrs. this day and date abovesaid In
Obedience to an Ordr. of Court bearing date the 7th May 1684
As Witness or: hands ds   ELIAS X WILSON
                                                              THOMAS ⊙ NEWMAN

     This within Inventory was sworne to before me
   by ye Apprisers June 28th 1684
          GEORGE TAYLOR
   Recordatr primo die Septembris Anno 1684

pp.   September Court Anno 1684
42-   IN THE NAME OF GOD Amen I HARMAN SKELDERMAN being sick of body yett
43   thanks be unto God of perfect memory doe make and ordaine this my last Will
        and Testament in manner and forme as followeth.
   First I comend my Soule unto the hands of the Almighty God my Maker, hopeing to be
saved by the merritts of Jesus Christ my Redeemer and my body to the Christian buriall
& for my temporall goods I dispose of them as followeth
   I give and bequeath unto my loveing Wife all my household goods & cattells & hoggs &
a horse & young mare and if a young mare lives to Increase, that then each of my Children to have a Mare Colt out of said Mares increase
   2dly I doe alsoe give and bequeath unto my Children Six hundred acres of land where
now I live to be equally devided between them when they shall come to age and if any
of them should die before that time that then the land to be equally devided between
them as aforesaid; And if that my children should all die before that they should come
to age then the said land I bequeath unto my loveing Wife whome I make whole & sole
Executrix to pform this my last Will and Testamt. In Witness whereof I have hereunto
sett my hand and seale this 12th of March 1683/4
Signed & Sealed in the presence of us   HARMAN SKELDERMAN
      ALEXR. DONIPHANN,
         JNO. ⊙ GARTON, SUSANA ⫴HAMMON
   Proved & recorded in the County Court of Rappa 3d day 7ber 1684
   We the Subscribers doe depose & say that we saw ye abovenamed HARMAN SKELDER-
MAN Signe Seale & Deliver this above for his last Will and Testamt. And that the said
Testator was at the same time of pfect mind and memory to the best of or: knowledge
                                                         ALEXR. DONIPHAN
                                                         JNO. ⊙ GARTON
                                                         SUSANA ⫫ HAMON

   Sworne to in Court   Test WM. COLSTON Cl Cur

pp.   Rappa. County March 8th 1683/84
43-   AN INVENTORY and Apprisemt. of the Estate of Mr. JNO. MOTLEY deced the date
45   first written   THE CATTLE
        To 13 cowes, 7 yearling cattle, 2: 7: yeare old Steers, 2: small Bull, 5 Steers 4 yeare
old, a small horse, a Mare called Jenny; an old Cart Horse, cart wheels & harness, one

hhd. Tob: conta. neal; 14 Ells Course sheeting; 14 yards narrow blew; 11 yds LIncy Woolsey, one peice Cullered dimity, 49 Ells narrow wt. course linen, 26 ells Hambarough Linen, 19 ells Garman narow dowlis, 20 ells broad ditto; 11 yds Kersey, 18 yards Kersey, 8 yards Serge, one peice of fine Serge, 75 Ells Course Canvas, 28 Ells fine broad Canvas, 10 ells course Holland, 10 Ells broad fine dowlis; 12 Buck Skins at 40; 13 doe Skins at 25; a parcell old stockins; 4 paire cours ditto, one paire good wosted ditto; 1 Ell fine Issingham holland; 1 pr cours small sheets; 1 old Canvas flock bed, 2 ruggs & bedsted, one old feather bed, 2: old Ruggs & bedsted; 3 old gunns, parcell Roanock, 6 old diaper napkins & table cloath; 3 lb. shott, a small bail cotton weick & a caske soape; 4 old Chests, a good table & old Table & old form, 4 old chaires & couch very old, 2 old brass kettles & a Skillett, 5 old iron potts & pr Pott hooks, a very old Iron kettle with a hole in ye bottom, one old fraying pan; 2 very old ladles; 2 reap hookes very old; 3 old pailes & 6 old trayes, 4 old wedges, one old pestell, an old porringr., one old brand axes & two old Spancells & a hammer, a parcell new nailes, 3 bushells of Salt

   A list of Debts: ARTHUR ONBEY by Bill; JAMES TOMPKINS, JAMES ORCHARD 2 bushells of Salt; WM. PAYNE a bushell Salt; FRANCIS STONE a bushell of salt; GILES MATHEWS a bushell of Salt; JNO. DEANE, Capt. LORD, Capt. GEORG PURVIS, JNO. BONKITT a deer skin; ROBT. GAINES one doe Skin; WM. BROWN a buck Skin; XPHER THOMAS by Exec. in Sheriffs hands; KNIGHT RICHARDSON by Bill, JNO. BUTCHER p ordr. Court; Servt. boy 7 years to serve by Indenture; 2 pr Childrens shoes & one pr mens; a very old candlestick & Chaffin dish, 2 old grubing hoes, one old Grind stone; one old Spitt; one pr pott racks, 1 old Iron bound case bottles

   We the Subscribers do find the goods to be very well rated according to Invoyce as witness or: hands   FRANCIS STONE
                                                     WILLIAM CLAPHAM

   In Obedience to an Ordr. of the Worll. Court of Rappa County bearing date the Eighth day of March Ano 1683/4 wee the Subscribrs. have apprized the Estate of the abovesaid JNO. MOTLEY deceased to three and thirty thousand eight hundred & fifty four pounds of Tob: to the best of or: Judgmt. as Witness or: hands the date abovesd.
                                                     RICH: BRAY
                                                     WILLIAM CLAPHAM

   The Execr. of the said Estate and alsoe the Apprisers were sworne before me this 8th March 1683/4

                                                     GEORGE TAYLOR
   May the 7th 1684 WM. CLAPHAM did this day in open Court make Oath to the truth of this Inventory & that it was the whole Estate of JNO. MOTLEY deced & herein mentioned that was exhibited to him

                              Test   WM. COLSTON, Cl Cur

   Recordatr xx5th die 7bris Ano 1684

pp.   AN INVENTORY of the Estate of EVAN MORGAN as it was apprized this 14th June
45-   Anno Dom 1684
45   3 old Cowes 13 yeares old a apeice & calves, 3 cowes and calves, 1 young cow
          lame of her hooffs; 3 young barran cowes 2 yeares old; 4 yearling, one red Steer & 1 brown pyed Steere; one red Bull, one white horse & black mare; one young Snip shotten Mare & foale, one young black horse 4 yeare old, One man Servt., one man Servt., one Woman servt., one Servt. boy called THOMAS HAMMEN, 31 lb. Pewter, one brass kettle warming pan, pistelles & morter & a small brass kettle all old brass, a parcell of old Iron ware & 2 pestells, 2 wedges, a box smoothing Iron all togeather, foure cripled guns, two pistolls & old Rapier, 12 iron potts, one iron kettle, one frying pann, 1

driping pann, one table leafe & form, a parcell of Lumber, 2 chests, pr. Stillard; 3 Feather Beds & boulster & pillows with their rugge & blankett; a parcell of small empty
caske, a small table & couch, a parcell of old books, 2 small Rimletts, one sifter for
meale, pd to JNO. NORINGTON for JNO ROBINSONs passage (1600)   Total 22152
   one young stone horse 2 yeares old that hath not been seen since the fall to be ac-
comptable for when found
   A Just Inventory of what was brought to or: sight of the Estate of EVAN MORGAN As
witness or: hands   FRANCIS THORNTON
                                                WILLIAM STROTHERS
                                                THOMAS ARNOLD
                                                ADAM WEFFENDALL

   These Apprizers sworne before me to the Just Appraizmt. of this Estate, likewise the
Widdow to EVAN MORGAN before me for a Just discovery of the same
                                                ANTHONY SAVAGE

   Recordatr xx5 die 7bris Anno 1684

p.   In Obedience to power from Col: WM. LOYD wee the Subscribrs. have Inventoried
46   & apprised the small Estate of MARGT. POWERS, late deced as foll:
          One sorry fistaload horse, a gown well worn & two old peticoats; 3 peticoats, a
pr old boddes & an old Gowne, 3 yds of St. Martin lace; one old smock, 3 peices of head
linnen, a parcell small linen, a parcell of Silk thread, an old white Vest, 4 old blew
aprons, an old Rush hatt and a small Chip baskett; REES EVANS obligation WM. SARGENTs
Executors; an old sow & a barrow of a yeare & a halfe old   Total 1066
                                                HEZEKIE E COLLEDGE
                                                RALPH WHITING

   Estate of MARGT. POWERS To a Coffin sheet; Digging ye grave & buriall, To her bill is
due   Total 1600
   Errors Excepted 4d 7bris 1684
   Recordatr xx5 die 7bris 1684

pp.   IN THE NAME OF GOD Amen. I DANIELL GAINES of the Parish of Sittenburne in
47-   the County of Rappa: being in good health of body & of sound & perfect memory
48   Praise be therefore given to Almighty God do make and ordaine this my last
          Will and Testament in manner and forme following; That is to say, First & prin-
cipally I commend my soul into the hands of Almighty God hopeing through the merits
death & passion of my Saviour Jesus Christ to have full & free pardon and forgiveness
of all my sins and to inherit everlasting life and my body I commit to the Earth to be
decently buried at the discretion of my Executrx. hereafter named. And as touching the
disposition of all such worldly Estate as it hath pleased God to bestow upon me I give &
dispose thereof as followeth
   Imprimis. It is my will that all my Debts that I justly owe to any man be well & truely
paid & in the first place that the Orphants of Colnll. JOHN CATLETT deced to be paid out of
the negroes and other goods that did belong to the sd Colnll. CATLETs Estate the Negroes
& Goods to be pd. as they were appraised to me as may appear by Inventory
   Item I give & bequeath unto my Son, BERNARD, all my land that I now live upon to
him & his heires lawfully begotten & that he shall not let sell or mortgage any part or
parcell of the same so longe as his two Sisters, MARGRET & MARY, or their heires be
alive. It is my will that if all my Children die without heires of their bodyes then my
land to fall to my Grandson, JOHN SMYTH, & to his heires forever
   Item I give to my Daughter, MARY, the Mare colt that now sucks on my Mare Betty and

all her encrease to her & her heires for Ever

Item. It is my will that the Mare Heyfer & hogs that I have given to my Grandson in Law, JOHN SMITH, be & remaine to his proper use forever

Item. It is my Will that the first living Child that my Negro Cate doth bring be given to my Daughter, MARGRETT, and to her heires for ever & if it lives to the age of three yeares to be in lieu of a man Servant, otherwise to be in no stead

Item. I do give to my Son, BERNARD, my Silver hilted sword & Belt & my Seale Ring

Item. I give unto my deare & loveing Wife, MARGRET, one third of all my Estate in lieu of her Dowre

Item. My will is that the other two parts of my Estate be deviced between my three Children, BERNARD, MARGRET & MARY and no part of it be apprised but to be inventoried & delivered in kind

Item. It is my will that my Daughter, MARGARET, have a good feather bead & furniture at my death in full of her part of my bedding

Item. It is my will that my Daughter, MARY, have the use of so much housing & land as she needs soe long as she continued unmarried

Item. It is my will that as soone as it can a man Servant be bought with Tobacco for my Daughter, MARGARET, in part of he porcon

Item. It is my will that my Wife, Son BERNARD, and Daughter MARY keep their shares together for their menteynance doing their best by their Endeavours to Encrease the same as long as my Wife continues a Widdow or so long as either of my Children continue unmarried and at the day of Marriage of my Wife or of either of my Children, then my Childrens part to be delivered them in kind

Item. My will is that my two Children, BERNARD & MARY, have as many things apeice out of my Estate as my Daughter, MARGARET, hath had already & the rest to be devided between them equally by my loveing Kinsman, JOHN CATLETT, & Sons in Law, JOHN SMYTH and RALPH ROWZEY, and not to go to Law one with the other

Item It is my will that my Estate be inventoryed within ten dayes after my decease

Item. I give to my deare & loveing Wife Twenty Shillings to buy her a Mourning Ring to ware for my sake & to my two Daughters each of them a Ring of Ten Shillings price

Item. It is my will that if I die haveing no tobacco in my house that my Servants bee & remaine together till they make a good crop of Arenoco Tobacco out of which my Wife having first taken her thirds, then my Son BERNARD & Daughter MARY have out of the rest each of them as much as my Daughter, MARGRETT, hath already then if any be remaining over & above to be devided equally between them all three

Item. It is my will that my Children have their Estate at the death or day of Marriage of my Wife whether they be of age or not

Item It is my will that the Children of Colnll. JOHN CATLETT remaine with my Wife till they come of age, if my Wife continue unmarried

Item. I nominate & appoint my dear and loveing Wife my sole Executrix of this my last Will and Testamt. and Guardian to my Children so longe as she lives a Widdow. In Witness whereof I the sd DANIELL GAINES to this my last Will & Testamt. do sett my hand & Seale this Eighteenth of August in the yeare of our Lord One thousand Six hundred Eighty & two

Signed Sealed & delivered and declared   DANIELL GAINES
  this to be my last Will & Testamt. in the
  presence of WM. W MURROW,
      JOHN CATLETT, WM. W BROWNE

Wee the Subscribers do hereby testifie and declare upon or: Oaths that wee did see Capt. DANLL. GAINES within menconed signe seale & deliver this within menconed as his last

Will & Testamt. & that he was then in perfect sence & memory to the best of our knowledge
                                                        WM. *WB* BROWNE
                                                        JOHN CATLETT
                                                        WM. *W* MURROW

Jurati sunt in Cur Com Rappa. 1. die 8bris Ano 1684 et Recodatr 16

pp.   IN THE NAME OF GOD Amen. I WALTER STALLARD being sick & weake but of good
48-   & perfect sence & memory & calling to minde the certainty of death & the un-
49   certainty of my life do make this my last Will & Testamt. making void all other
        Wills by me before made & this to be looked on and taken for my last.
Imprimis. I commit my Soul into the hands of God that gave it in sure & certaine hope
of a joyfull resurrection by the merits of my sweet Redeemr. Jesus Christ & my Body to
be buried at the discretion of my Exetrs. hereafter named & for what Estate it hath
pleased God of his goodness to bestow on me I give & bequeath as followeth
I will that all my just Debts that I owe to any iman be well & justly paid
Item. I give unto my Son, SAMLL., & Daughter, SARAH, all my land, houseing & orchards to them & to their lawfull heires to be equally devided by honest men and, it
being devided, my Son to have his choice, and one of them die not haveing issue as
above sd, then the other to enjoy the whole to his heires or to her heires for Ever
Item. I give unto my Son & Daughter each of them two Cowes & all their female En-
crease to be delivered at the age of 21 yeares or day of Marriage which shall first
happen
Item I give to my Son & Daughter abovesaid one Heifer, two cow yearlings & the first
cow calfe that any of my cowes doe bring together with their female Encrease to them
& their heirs as abovesd.
Item I give my bay horse to my Son, SAMUELL, & to his heires
Item I give to my Daughter. SARAH, my black horse called Ball & to her heires for
Ever
Item I give to my Son one Pottanger & one pewter dish to be pd when he comes att age
Item I give to my Daughter one Pottanger & one Pewter Salt to be pd her when she
comes of age
Item the rest of my Estate I give to my loveing Wife together with the male colts, bull
calves that come from my Childrens Mares & Cowes for the paymt. of my Debts &
bringing up of my Children
Item I constitute & appoint my loveing Wife, WINIFRED, my sole Exectrx. of this my
last Will & Testamt. In Testimony of this & what is wrote on the other side, I have sett
my hand & seale this 28th of December 1683
Signed Sealed & Delivered & Declared
this to be his last Will & Testamt.
                                                WALTER X STALLARD
        JOHN EVANS,
        GEO: *P* PEACHEY, GEO: *Ce* ANDREWS
Wee the Subscribrs. do hereby testifie & declare upon Oath that we did see the within
named Testator signe seale & deliver the within menconed as his last Will & Testamt. &
that he was then in perfect sence & memory to the best of our knowledge
                                                GEO: *P* PEACHEY
                                                GEO: *O* ANDREWS

Jurati sunt in Curia Com Rappa: 1 die Octobris ano 1684

pp.
49-
50

IN THE NAME OF GOD Amen. I JOHN EVANS of Sittenburn Parish in the County of Rappa: being sick and weake of body but of perfect memory of minde blessed be God therefore do constitute & make this my last Will & Testamt. in manner & forme following

Imprimis. I give my soule into the hands of Almighty God my Creator trusting & hopeing for salvation only by the merits of Jesus Christ my Saviour & Redeemer & for my body I order it to be decently buried by my Exectrx. herafter named as soone as she shall think it convenient after my decease not doubting but I shall receive it againe being raised by the mighty power of God at the generall Resurrection & so both body & soul united I shall enjoy the blessed presence of God to all Eternity; And as for my worldly goods & Estate both reall & personall which it hath pleased God to bestow upon me, I give & bequeath in manner & forme following

I give & bequeath all the land I am possessed of to my two Sons, 1 JOHN EVENS & WM. EVENS to be equally devided between them both for quantity & quality, the devision to be made when my Son, JOHN, shall accomplish & attaine the age of one & twenty yeares & in case the one shall decease before his full age the other shall succeed in his inheritance

Item I give & bequeath to each of my Children a Mare & all their encrease the youngest Mare I give unto my Son, JOHN, the other to my Son, WILLIAM, as also I give to each of them a Cow withall their encrease, my Son, JOHN, to have a Cow called Mealy Nose, my Son, Wm:, shall have a black Cow called Slow. My Children I order to stay & live with their Mother till they attaine to the age of Nineteen yeares each of them

Item I give and bequeath to my loveing Father in Law, Mr. WM. PEALE, a case of pistolls and holsters

Item I give and bequeath unto my loveing Brother, MARTIN JOHNSON, a Chest which I had of him as alsoe a gun which I had of him and a Castor hatt

Item I give unto my God Child, MARGRETT WARD, Daughter of BRYANT WARD, a Cow calfe to be given her by my Executrix & the first Cow Calfe yt. falls

All the rest of my goods & chattells after my debts are satisfied I give and bequeath wholly and solely unto my well beloved Wife, ELIZABETH EVANS, whome I constitute and appointe my sole Executrix to this my last Will and Testament, as also Guardian to my Children. In Witness whereof and to all these fore mentioned premises I have hereunto put my hand and Seale the twenty ninth of January 1683
Signed Sealed Delivered & pnounced to be
my last Will & Testament in the prsence of us: JOHN EVANS
       RICHD. R WEST
       THOMAS JOHNSON, WILLM. HEATHER
Wee the Subscribers doe hereby testify & declare that the wthin mentioned is the last Will and Testamt. of JNO. EVANS within named and that we did see the said EVANS signe seale and Delivr. this to be his last Will & Testamt. and that he was then in perfect sence and memory at the signing & sealing thereof to the best of or: knowledg
                                             WILL HEATHER
                                             RICHD. R WEST

Jurati sunt in Cur Com Rappa 1 die 8bris Anno 1684

pp.
50-
51

August the 20th 1684
In Obedience to an Ordr. of Rappa. County Court held the Six one thousand Six hundred eighty and fouwer, wee ye Subscribers have apprised the Estate of THOMAS HARPER deced
Imrs. Four cowe yearlings, five steer yearlings, eight barren cowes, six cows and

calfes, one stear of five yeare, one of fower year, one Bull of three yeare old, one mare of six yeare old, one young mare and Colt, one feather bed Rugg & two boulsters, one old feather bed bouldster, two pillows and new rigg & 2 blanketts, one table & forme & one old chaire, three old chests, one old box, three iron potts, fifty two pounds old pewter, two insufficient hhds. one quarter Casq., one powdering tubb; three old wedges not seen, one long gunn, a parcell of old books, one old hand saw, three paire pott hooks, one old Glass, one old Couch, one iron pestle, two old brass kettles, one skillet, a paire of brass candlesticks, two old butter tubbs, one servant boy about six yeare old Total 16444
  By the Will there is given to JOHN HARPER one Gun and one Servant boy which amounts to   Remaining 15244
  Which divided into fower equall shares   3811

                    PARNALL PERRY
                    THO: EDMONDSON
                    JOHN WATERS

Sworne in the Court of Rappa 1st Octobr: 1684 by
Subscribers and recorded

p.   9ber Court Ano 1684
51   IN THE NAME OF GOD Amen. I WM. GRIFFIN of Cittenborne Parish in the County
        of Rappa., Planter, being very sick and weake of body but in perfect sence and memory blessed be God doe make my last Will and Testament as followeth:
  First I bequeath my soule to God that gave it & my body to be decently buried at the discretion of my surviving friends hopeing for a joyfull Resurrection of the same in & through the meritts of Jesus Christ
  As for my worldly Estate I do dispoe of it as followeth:
  First I give unto my Son, WILLIAM, 225: of acres of that land bought of MR. MOTT and to have it next the River, and ye rest of that tract being 125: acres to my Son, JOHN, as also I bequeath to my Son, JOHN, a tract of land ye 75: acres bought of JAMES JACKSON wch makes the number of given to my Son, JOHN, equall with my Son, WILLIAM. And my will is that if it please God either of my Sonns die without issue, the Survivr. to enjoy the whole Estate
  2dly. I give and bequeath two thirds of my personall Estate to my Sonns, WM. & JOHN, & the other third part I give to my Wife
  3dly. My Will is that both my Sonns live and remaine with my Wife untill they arive at the age of twenty one yeares if she remaines a Widow, but If she marrys then my will is that they shall be free at the age of eighteen yeares
  Lastly, I do appointe my welbeloved Wife, JANET, to be my sole Exectrx. of this my last Will and Testamt. and doe hereby revoke all other Wills and Testamts. heretofore made. In Witness whereof I have hereunto sett my hand and seale this first day of Janry. 1683
Signed Sealed & Delivrd. in the presence of
        JAMES HARRISON,   WILLIAM GRIFFIN
        JAMES JACKSON
  Wee whose names are undr. written doe depose that we heard the Testator publish and declare this to be his last Will & Testamt. And that he was in perfect sence & mimorie when he did it   JAMES HARRISON
                                                  JAMES JACKSON
  Proved in Court by the Oaths of Mr. JAMES HARRISON & Mr. JAMES JACKSON, on the 5th day of November Ano 1684

pp.   IN THE NAME OF GOD Amen. I HENRY WHITE of the County of Rappa being sick
51-   and weake of body yett of perfect sence and memory doe make this my last Will
52   and Testamt. in manner and form following
          Imps. I bequeath my Soule to God that gave it me and my body to the Dust in
hopes of a blessed resurrection through my Lord and blessed Saviour Jesus Christ and
as for my Temporl: Estate I doe dispose of as in this manner
   Item I bequeath unto my Daughter, ARABELLA. all my lands that I have and doe enjoy
in the County and elswhere to her and her heires for Ever; And in case of her death
witthout issue, then I bequeath my land to my beloved Wife, DORCAS, and her heires for
Ever
   Item I bequeath all my psonall estate to my beloved Wife, DORCAS, And doe make & ordaine her my Executrix of this my last Will and Testament revoaking all former Wills by
me had & made and doe declare this and non other to be my last Will and Testament. In
Witness whereof I have hereunto sett my hand and seale this 14th day of February Ano
1683/4
Signed Sealed & published in prsence of
          ROBERT MOSS,   HENRY WHITE
             JOHN P GOOGE
   Wee the Subscribrs. doe hereby testifie & declare that we did see the within named
Testator signe seale & delivr. this within written to be his last Will and Testament and
that he was then in perfect sence and memory at the signing and Sealing hereof to the
best of or: knowledge And &c.

                                        ROBERT MOSS
                                        JOHN P GOOGE
   Proved in Court by the Oaths of ROBT. MOSS & JOHN GOOGE the 5th Nobr. 1684 and recorded 24th same month & yeare

p.   THE LAST WILL and TESTAMT. of JOHN MAFFITT, Wheelright, of the Parish of
52   Sittingborne in the County of Rappa, he being in his right and perfect sences.
          First I bequeath laying my Soule at the ffeet of Christ seeking for mercy my
body to be buried with Christian buriall
   Imprs. for my land to be equally devided in three parts to my Wife one part dureing
her said life and after he decease to my Son; likewise my Daughter to have a part
dureing her life and after he decease to my Son aforesaid or his heires for Ever, But he
having no issue to the longest life of them all, But as for my stock and goats to be
equally between them; my Wife to be Cheife and Executrix & manager of all as long as
she remaines a Widdow, But if she be changing her condition in marrying, then for
each to have their shares if they demand them. In Witness whereof I have put my
hand this Twenty Sixth day of March in the year of or: Lord One thousand Six hundred
and Eighty two
Teste MARY MASON,   the Marke of
       JOHN MASON, THO: WEBLEY   JOHN X MAFFITT
   I the Subscribr: doe declare that I did see the wthin named Testator signe & publish
this within written as his last Will and Testamt. And that he was then in perfect sence
and memory to the best of his knowledg
                                        JOHN MASON
   Swore to me in Court by MASON 5th of 9ber 1684 & Record 25th

pp.   THE INVENTORY and Apprisemt. of the Estate of Mr. JNO. GIBSON Inventoryed and
52-   apprised the 6th day Nobis 1684 & according to an Ordr. of the Worll. Court of the
54   County of Rappae: bearing date the 3d day of Septembr: 1684 by ROBERT PLAY,
       ROBT. MOSS & EDWD. MOSELEY

Imprs. His Cattle: 7 cows &1 heiffer of 3 yeare old, 3 calves of the first yeare, 2 steers
of 4 yeare old, 3 Draft Steers, 4 cowes of a yeare and halfe old; 1 Steer 9 yeare old and
one Cow, 1 Steer 4 yeare old; 1 Steer 3 yeare old, 1 Mare of 16 yeare old & her colt, One
horse of 6 yeare old his Riding Horse, one young horse bridle and sadle, one young
horse 2 yeare old runing in the woods

His Apparell. One Sute of cloaths, Coat breeches & wast coate, 2 wast coats and one pr
drawers of Dimity, 1 hatt 2 brushes and one pr gloves, books, a parcell of books, a pare
of scales with their weights, bedding, one feather bed one bowlster a pr. sheets coverled and an old ticking, one old bed & boulster, 2 sheets and a coverled, 1 old Table &
forme, 5 old chaires & a bedsted, one feather bed, one rugg, one bowlster & pillow, a pr.
of blanketts & an old bed lick; one old flock bed & bedsted and another old bed with it
and what belongings to it; old curtains, an old Coate &wastcoate & a cider cloath, 2 table
cloathes, 1/2 dozen napkins & a pillow beer; 3 sheets, one old coper kettle, one carbine
gun, a pcell of old lumber, Iron & 2 old Candlesticks, a parcell of pewter contaying 78
pounds at 9 lb. p pound; one flaggon, 3 Candlesticks & 2 salts; 3 iron potts, 12 pott racks,
one spitt, a driping pan and an iron pestle, one looking glass, parcell of old lumber, 2
bagges, a grind stone and an old forme, a Servant haveing two months to serve and his
Comand cloaths to be paid him, forty hoggs great & small runing in the woods, one Bill
of Debt p JOHN HILL , 2 hhds Tob weight, clean old toba: hhds, one old pr of cart wheels

                              Suma total   21815

This Inventory taken & apprizmt. made the day and year first above written per
                              ROBERT PLEY
                  ROBERT MOSS   EDWARD MOSELEY
Sworn befor me this 3d day of Novembr. ano 1684
                              HEN: AWBREY

Recorded 25th 9ber 1684

pp.   AN INVENTORY and Apprizmt. of the Estate of Mr. GEORG JONES deced taken this
54-   18th day of 7ber 1684 by Capt. GEORG TAYLOR, Capt. SAMUEL BLOMFEILD, Mr.
56   JAMES HARRISON and Mr. WM. MOSS

       Imprs. To one feather bed boulster & bleu rugg, one long table & forme, 2
smaller tables, 1 very old cubbard, 2 great old chests, 15 old leather chaires, 4 other
leather chaires

In the Parlor: one old feather bed flock bowlster & rugg, one old feather bed bowlster
rugg, 2 chests one very old, 1 cubbard, one little table and drawer, one pr andirons with
brass heads, a parcell of old cloaths, one broad cloath coat lined, 26 ells fine 3 in Dowlis,
43 ells broad Dowlis 8 ells Canvas, a parcell old curtaines, parcell Diaper table cloaths &
napkins, 1 pr holland sheets, 2 pr sheets, 4 pr & one sheet of canvas, 2 old pillo beers, 2
canvas table cloaths, 1/2 whited brown thread; about 1 lb. & 1/2 brown thread; 189 lb.
pewter, silver tankard, parcell old books, 2 old brass candlesticks, one old brass kettle &
old skimer; 2 pr andirons, 1 pr iron racks, iron spitts, 3 iron potts & two pr pott hooks,
one old Skillet and old warming pan; one very old frying pan; one very old table in the
Kitchen; 12 very old Couches, one old chest; Hamo a Turk 7 yeares to serve by Indenture
Secundus a Negro man, Negro girle Black Bess 12 yeares old; 2 Negro women very old
over at POPLER NECKE.

An Acct. of the Cattle - Cowes, Calves, 6 oxen steers, heifers, yearling Steers, yearling

Bulls, 8 bulls, 2 iron potts and pott racks one pr old Cart wheeles & grind Ston, one old
Ginn   Total 26161

In Obedience to an Ordr. of Rappa County Court bearing date the 3d September 1684
Wee the Subscribrs. have apprised that part of the Estate of Mr. GEORG JONES deced that
was prsented to or: veiw by the Relict and Admintrx. of ye said JONES, As Witness or:
hands this 18th day of 7ber 1684

    Sworne before me   GEORG TAYLER
    7ber 18th 1684   SAML. BLOMFEILD
    HEN: AWBREY   WM. /X\ MOSS

List of Debts due to the Estate of Mr. GEORG JONES deced taken by us
3 Mares and Colts by their sides; the Debts: 2 Sadle horses, 1 horse of 2 year old, 1 old
blind horse, 35 head of hoggs   Page 1st goods   30751
                                      Page 2nd goods   26161
                  Sum totall   108308
                GEORG TAYLER   WM. /X\ MOSS
                SAMLL. BLOMFEILD   JAMES HARRISON

The list of Debts Horses & hoggs apprized by
Capt. GEORG TAYLER & Mr. WM. MOSS the Subscribers
List of Tobaccoes of the Sumes of Tobacs due unto Mr. GEORGE JONES (Vlzt.) 1684 (two
columns.   Totall Sume 38996
3 Mares and Colts by their sides, 2 Sadle horses, 1 horse 2 yeares old, 1 old blind horse,
35 head of hoggs great and small

                           HONORIA JONES

Recorded 26th 9ber Ano 1684

pp.   At a Court held for Rappa County Novembr. 5th 1684
56-   Mr. JNO. RICE, Mr. JNO. BAYLEY, Mr. SAML. BAYLEY, Mr. JOSHUA DAVIS are by
57   this Court apponted to make enquire into the Estate of Mr. JNO. WEIRE dec. Son
       of Majr. JNO. WEIRE deced haveing regard to his deced Father's Will and make
report thereof in writing under their hands to this Court how much the said Estate doth
amount to

                 Copia Test   WM. COLSTON Cl Cur
In pursuance whereof we have devided the said Estate by the Inventory in three equal
parts & the third part is as followeth (Vizt) In Cattle great & small; in Guns; in Hoggs, in
holland Sheets, in one third of Eleaven English hhds. of French Salt; in flaxxen sheets,
large Diapr. Table cloaths; look glasses, diapr. napkins, one third of toba: hdds.
amounting to 106695; large flaxen table cloath, 1/2 of 4 Negroes; 1/2 of a mulatto boy;
1/2 of England Servants; to feathr. beds; bowlsters, pillows, sheep, horses, in blanketts,
mares, sarge curtains, new great turkey chaires, candlesticks, salts, tankards, flaggins,
chambr. potts, in pottingrs. and a cup neat weight of dishes; in plates new; in plate
silver, brass kettles, iron potts, fry pans

                 Examined and Auditted by us
                 JOHN RICE   JOHN BAYLY
                 SAML. BAYLEY   JOS. DAVIS

Recorded xx7 day Novr. 1684

p.   March Court 1684/5
57   An Appraismt. made by us the Subscribers by Order of Coln. JOHN STONE of the
       Estate of Mr. GEORGE SOUTHIN deced taken the 15th day of January 1684/5
Imprs. Two cowes & calves, one young bull, one little poore horse, two old tables & a

forme, one old branding Iron, two old Bedsteads, ten very old chaires, one very old
feather bed curtains & vallances & two canvas pillows; to one very old tattered side sadle
& save guard, one old brass kettle, one old iron pott, 2 small pott racks, one small dripping pan, one very old patched frying pan, two small tinn sauce pans, 1 pare of tongues
1 old gun, one very old falling ax & to the fferey boat, one old Piggin, 1 old bed cords, 1
old wooden candle stick; one Lanthorne, one small payle, small parcell of very old
pewter, 2 very old Brushes, 2 old torne sifters, one spade. Suma totalis   7676

                                           ARTHUR SPICER
                                           BOWEN RADFORD
                                           DAVID STERNE

Recorded March 22th 1684/5

p.   March the 2d 1684/5.
58   AN INVENTORY of the Estate of Capt. JOHN ROLT deced as followeth
          One Feather head courtaines & vallances, 1 bitt of a coverlet & one peice of a
blankett; 2 chests, 1 brass kettle, 1 iron pott, 1 pewter dish & one bason; 1 spitt; 1 old
trunk, 3 broken chaires, 1 tin dripping pan, 1 pare of andirons, 1 rack, 1 fire shovell, 1
pare tongues, 1 andirons, 1 ladle, 1 forke, 1 cross cut saw, 1 warming pann, 1 cowe &
one calfe
          Recorded March 5th 1684/5

p.   The Appraismt. of the Estate of WALTER SCOTT deced
58   A new Kersey coat & breeches, a Chest, an old hand kertchu   314
                                           WM. SMITH
                                           JOHN A ADAMS
The above appraisers sworne before me this 15th day of February 1684/5
                                           WM. LLOYD

Record March 5th 1684/5

pp.   IN THE NAME OF GOD Amen. I DOMINICK RICE being sick of body but of perfect
58-   minde & memory doe make this my last Will & Testamt. as for followeth disanul-
59   ling all former Wills by me made
          Imprs. I do bequeath my soule to God who gave it me hopeing in Jesus Christ
my Mediator for Salvacon at the last day & in him only doe I put my Trust, wth my body
to convenient Christian buriall
     It. I do give unto WM. CASTOR, JOHN & ANN TUNE, the Children of JAMES TUNE each of
them one young Ewe & to the sd WM. my Broad Cloath suitt
     It. I do give unto my Son in Law, THO: DUE, my Stuff coat & breeches & my Rapier
     It. I do give unto my Son in Law, MARKE TUNE, my Gunn
     It. I do give unto my Son in Law, ANDW. DUE, Twenty Shill. to buy him a Ring
     It. I do give unto my Wifes Neice, JANE DUNCOMBE, one young (blank) of three years
old & the increase to be delivered her in May next
     It. I do give unto my well beloved Wife, ANN, two small gold rings
     It. I doe give to the over seers of my Will Twenty Shillings to each of them to buy each
of them a Ring
     It. I do give to my Son, STEPHEN RICE, all my lands, five hundred acres being upon
ST.JAMES POINT in CHOPTANK in MARYLAND and Three hundred & fifty acres more wch
I bought of MATHEW KELLY & IGNATIUS WHITE & called STONY HILL; and Three hundred
acres lying neare FARNHAM CREEK where JOHN PEACOCK now liveth & joying to it wch
I have entered in the SECRETARYS OFFICE and desire the overseers of this my Will to

Escheat the sd land to my Son, STEPHEN

It. I do order & appoint my well beloved Wife, ANN, & my Son, STEPHEN, my only Exe-cutrs. & doe give all ye remaining part of my Estate unto them

It. I do order and appoint that my Son, STEPHEN, be sent to IRELAND to my Father when is five years old there to be Educated so long as his Grand Father shall think fitt and what I have given him to remaine in the hands of his Mother untill he comes to the age of Seventeen security being given for it, but in case the sd STEPHEN should dye be-fore he come to the age of Seventeen what I have here given him to come to his Mother if she be then living, but if not then to fall to my Eldest Sisters Eldest Son in IRELAND.

It. I do order & appoint my good friends, Colnl. WM. LOYD, Capt. THO: MATHEWS & JOHN BAYLY to be my overseers in trust and to do their Endeavor to see that neither my Wife nor Child be wrong'd or abused either in body or Estate

In Witness of all & every pticular in this Will contained, I have hereunto set my hand & seale this Eight and Twentieth day of Octobr. 1683
Sind seald & deliverd in the presence of us

    JO: BAYLY,   DOMINICK RICE
    WM. BROCKENBURROUGH, ANDW: DEW

Wee the Subscribers did see Mr. DOMINICK RICE signe & seale this Will in perfect sence & memory Witness our hand the fourth day of March 1684/5

                  JNO. BAYLY
                  ANDREW DEW
                  WM. BROCKENBURROUGH

March 4th: 1684/5
Proved in Rappa Court by the Oaths of the Witnesses and recorded 11th

pp. January 25th: 1784/5
59-   IN THE NAME OF GOD Amen. I ROBT. PRITT of the County of Rappa in the Govern-
60   ment of Virginia though some distemper of body but sound & perfect memory
       praised be to God for it do here make & Ordaiane this as my last Will & Testamt.

Imprs. I give & bequeath my soule to God Almighty that gave it me & to Jesus Christ that died for me & to the Holy Gosts that sanctified me & my body to the Earth from whence it was taken & to be buried in Christian Buriall & my worldly goods as foll:

Imprs. I give & bequeath unto my well beloved Friend, RICHD. RICE SENR. and to his Son, RICHD. RICE JUNR. one seat of land contaying Two hundred acres of land wch. doth belong to me the sd ROBT. PRITT to be equally devided between him the sd RICHARD & his Son, this seat of land lying in Rappa County upon RAPPA. CREEK bounded as fol-loweth upon the land of ANDRW. BOYER, DUCKE THORNTON, JOSIAS LAWSON & FFRAN: SUTTLE

It. I give unto my Contry woman, ANN CONDON, Widdow, Five hundred pounds of Tobb:

It. I do hereby these prsents make ordaine & constitute & appointe these my Friends, RICHARD RICE SENR. & his Son, RICHD. RICE to be Executors Adminstrs. to take all my worldly goods as afore mentoned and to pay all my Legacys & to defray Christian buriall.

Also I request these my ffriends jointly and severally to ack and to demand of the under Sheriff of Rappa. Col. WM. TAYLER by name, for an Exect: taken out against Capt. JO: ROLT for two thousand pounds of Sweet sented Tobb: & four hundred weight Neet Pork: These also I give & bequeath unto RICHARD RICE SENR. & to his Son RICHARD RICE JUNR. This I assigne as my last Will and Testamt. as witness my hand & seale this day & yeare above written in the presence of these witnesses
Test THOROUGHGOOD PATE,   ROBT. PRID
    JERIMIA THORNTON his marke

Veria Copia Test THO: HOBSON JUNR. Cl. Cur Northampt. record
March 11th 1684/5
NORTHUMBERLAND ss. These are to certifie that on the 4th day of February THOROUGH-
GOOD PATE & JERIMIA THORNTON witnesses of the within Will did swear before Lt. Colnll.
SAMLL. SMYTH that the sd Will was the last Will & Testamt. of ROBT. PRITT deced, the
abovesd day being appointed for a Court for this County & no other Genl. appearing but
the above SMYTH

                                    Teste: THO: HOBSON Cl Cur

Record Test WM. COLSTON Cl Cur

pp.   IN THE NAME OF GOD Amen. I WM. FFRACK being of good & perfect memory do
60-   ordaine this as my last Will & Testamt. in manner & forme foll: Ffirst I give &
61   bequeath my soule in to the hands of Almighty God my blessed Creator & Re-
        deemer and my Body to be buried in Christian Burial at the hands of my Exect.
  Imprs. I give all my whole Estate both reall & personall unto my beloved Wife,
MARTHA FFRACK to be at her own disposing, my Debts & Legacies being pd.
  It. I give unto my man, ROBERT VINCENT, house & ground for to work upon for the
Terme of seven years if he please to worke on it himself, To have it rent free for the
full time aforemenconed
  It. I give unto my two Godsons, JOHN BROWNE and WM. PITMAN, to each of them a Cow
calfe
  And this is my full desire Revoking all other Wills and Testamts. In Witness of these
presents I sett my hand Aprill the 7th 1684
Test JOSEPH HENINGS,   WM. + FFRACK
    ROBT. VINCENT   his marke
  We the Subscribers doe depose & say that we saw the within named Testator signe seale
& publish this within Will as his last Will & Testamt. and that he was of perfect sence &
memory at the time of the sealing &c. thereof to the best of our knowledge and further
say not.

                                    JOSEPH HENINGE
                                    ROBT. VINCENT

  Proved in the County Court of Rappa by the Oaths of the Witnesses hereunto March the
5th 1684/5 & record 12th

p.   IN THE NAME OF GOD Amen the 15th: of February 1682 according to the Compu-
61   tacon of the Church of England I MARGRIT EDRINGTON of the Parish of Sitten-
        burne in the County of Rappa, Widdow, being of perfect memory and Remem-
brance praised be to God do make & ordaine this my last Will & Testamt. in manner &
forme foll:
  I bequeath my soule into the hands of Almighty god my maker hopeing that through
the meritorious death & passion of Jesus Christ my only Saviour & Redeemer to receive
ffree pardon & forgiveness of all my sins and as for my body to be buried in Christian
buriall at the discretion of my Exectr. hereafter named
  It. I give to my three Sons, JOHN JENNINGS & WM. JENNINGS & CHRISTOPHER EDRING-
TON, all my hogs & sheep & housall goods to be equally devided according to quantity &
quality
  It. I give unto my Son, WM. JENNINGS & CHRISTOPHER EDRINGTON, all my Mares &
horses that I die possessed with to be equally devided
  It. I give all my Cattle to my Son, CHRISTOPHER EDRINGTON, male and ffemale, & that if
either of my Sons, WM. or CHRISTOPHER, should die that all I give should goe to either of

them & their heires for ever

It. It is my will that my Sons should be at age at the age of Sixteen. It is my will that my Son, JOHN JENNINGS, my sole Exectr. of this my last Will & Testamt. Revokeing all other Wills & Testamts. In Witness whereof I have hereunto sett my hand and seale the day & yeare first above written

Test: FFRAN: STONE,				MARGT + ETHERINGTON
  ELIZ: STONE

I the Subscriber do depose & say that I saw this Testatrx. signe seale & publish this within Will as her last Will & Testamt. & that the sd Testatrx. was of perfect sence and memory at the signing & sealing thereof to the best of yor: Deponents knowledge & far: saith not

       FFRAN: STONE

Proved in the County Court of Rappa by the Oath of FFRAN: STONE this 4th day of March 1684/5

pp. April Court 1685
61- IN THE NAME OF GOD Amen. I THOMAS HERBERT being very sick and weak but of
62 sound & perfect memory Praise be to Almighty God for it, do make & ordaine this my last Will & Testament in manner and forme following

Imprimis. I bequeath my soule to God that gave it hoping that I shall receive salvation by & through the Merits of my blessed Lord & Saviour Jesus Christ and for my worldly Estate wch. the Almighty hath been pleased to bestow upon me I bequeath in manner & forme following

Item It is my will & desire that my just Debts be paid by my Exectr. hereafter named and that I have Christian buriall after his discretion to be buried where he shall think most convenient

It. It is my will & desire that after my Debts being paid & funerall charges that my Cozen, JOHN WATERS, have all & singular my Estate moveables & Immoveables and whatever doth of right appertaine unto me as being Execr. of Mrs. ELIZABETH CRASK deced, I do freely give unto my Cozen, JOHN WATERS, & his heires only one Cow & Calfe wch. I have at HENRY NEWTONs I give unto JOHN WATERS JUNR. to him & his heires both male & female

Lastly, it is my desire that JOHN WATERS SENR. be sole & whole Exectr: of this my last Will and Testament Revoking all Will or Wills wch. I have either made by Will or Verbally In Testimony whereof I have hereunto set my hand & seale this 8th: January 1684/5

Signed Sealed & Delivered in the presence of
  ELIZABETH B NEWTON,			THOMAS HERBERT
  FRANCES MOSS, WILLIAM M JONES

Rappa Court Aprill 1st: 1685. WM: JONES made Oath that THOMAS HERBERT was of sound & perfect memory at the signing & sealing of thie his last Will & Testamt. & that he saw him signe & seale the same

     WILLIAM M JONES

Proved in the County Court of Rappa by the Oath of WM. JONES

p. IN THE NAME OF GOD Amen. I JANE KING of the County of Rappa in Virginia
62 being sick & weak in body but of perfect sence & memory thanks be unto God for it do make & ordaine this my last Will & Testamt. in manner & forme following

Imprims. I give and bequeath my Soule to God that gave it me in certaine hopes of a

joyfull Resurrection at the last day in & through the merits of Jesus Christ my Redeemer my body to the ground from whence it came

It. After my Debts are satisfied, I give & bequeath my Estate as followeth. I give unto
my eldest Son, JOHN LOFLIN, Two pewter dishes & one Cow called by the name of Bunnie
with all her future increase

It. I give & bequeath unto my Son, ROBERT KING, one Heifer yearling with all her increase to him and his heirs for ever and one broad pewter dish and one pewter tankard

It. I do make & ordaine JOHN MILLS my whole & sole Exectr. of this my last Will & Testamt. into whose care & custody I do commit the tuitition of my two foresd Children and
what come & other provisions I shall be possessed of at the time of my decease I do give
towards the mentainance of them

It. What other houshold stuff I shall leave as also the Tobb: hanging and my wearing
cloaths I desire may be sold to pay my debts & defray my funerall charges and if any
over plus there be to be devided between my two said Children equally. In
confirmation whereof I have hereunto set my hand & seale this 24th day of January
Ano. 1684

Signed Sealed in presence of us

    THO: NEW,
    ROBT. his marke ⭕ WEBBER

    JANE KING H
    her marke

I the Subscriber doe depose & say that I did see the within named JANE KING signe
seale & publish this within menconed as her last Will & Testamt. and that she was then
in perfect sence & memory to the best of my knowledge As Witness my hand this 1st day
of Aprill Ano. 1685

            THO: NEW

Proved in Rappa County Court Aprill 1st 1685 by the Oath of THO: NEW & record
Sworne in Supia by ROBT. WEBBER May the 2d 1685 before
      Captt. GEO: TAYLER Justice

p.   IN THE NAME OF GOD Amen, the Eight day of April 1685. I ROGER WATERS being
63   sick & weak in body but of sound & perfect memory Praise be given unto God
    for ye same and knowing the uncertainty of this life on Earth & being desirous
to setle things in order do make this my last Will & Testamt. in manner & forme
following; that is to say, first & principally I commend my soul unto Almighty God my
Creator assuredly beleeving that I shall receive full pardon & free remission of all my
sins and be saved by the precious death & merits of my blessed Saviour & Redeemer
Jesus Christ & my body from the Earth from whence it was taken to be buried in such
decent & Christian manner as to my Executr. hereafter named shall be thought meet &
convenient, and touching such worldly Estate as the Lord in Mercy hath lent me my
Will & meaning is the same shall be imployed bestowed as hereafter by this my Will is
exprest.

Item I give & bequeath my horse, Trippilo, to Mrs. ANN GLASCOCK

It. I give & bequeath to FRANCES GLASCOCK a yew & a lamb

It. I give to JOHN OCKLY JUNR. a yew & a lamb

It. I give to JOHN OCKLY SENR. five hundred pounds of Tobacco

It. I give to NICHS. GLASCOCK five hundred pounds of Tobacco

It. I give unto MICHAEL SCURLOCK all my wearing cloths & my hatt

I do constitute & ordaine Mr. THOMAS GLASCOCK to be my full & whole Exectr. of this
my my last Will & Testament. I do also desire that my Exectr. will bury me in Christian
like manner in what place he shall think fitt and also to pay this my Legacys. I do also
give all that remaining part of my personall Estate to my Exectr. I do desire that JOHN

OAKLY do see that this my last Will & Testamt. be fulfilled, also it is my desire to have a funerall sermon preached by Doctr. DACRES In Witness whereunto I have sett my hand & seale the day & yeare above written

JOHN OACKLEY,   ROGER WATER
NICHO: CLARK

Wee the Subscribers, NICHO: CLARK aged forty years or thereabouts & JOHN OAKLEY aged forty years or thereabouts say that we saw Doctr. ROGER WATER being sound of mind & memory seale & deliver the annexed Will as his last Will & Testamt. and further say not   JOHN OAKLEY
                                                       RICHD. CLARK

Proved in Rappa County Court the 6th day of May 1685 by the Oaths of JOHN OAKLEY & NICHOLAS CLARK and record the 19th

pp. 63-64

IN THE NAME OF GOD Amen. I JOHN BARROW of the Parish of Sittenbourne of the County of Rappa being of sound mind & memory praised be God do make this my last Will & Testamt. in manner and forme following

I commending my Soul into the hands of Almighty God my most mercifull & loving Father in sure & certaine hope of the free pardon of my sins & obtainemt: of life everlasting in the Kingdom of heaven through the merits of Jesus Christ my Saviour & Redeemer my body I committ to the Earth to be decently Interred at the Discretion of my Exectrs. hereafter named

Item I give & bequeath to my Son, JOHANATHAN, and to his heires of his body lawfully begotten that part & parcell of land called the CABIN POINT begining at the Westward side of the cleared ground called the new ground & running down to the River along the branch and joyning to the land of PETER FFOXON & if my sd Son dye without heires as aforesd that then I give the land to him given to my Son, ALEXR. BARROW, & his heires

Item I give unto my Son, MOSES BARROW, & to the heires of his body lawfully begotten that tract or parcell of land beginning at the CART PATH in the East side of the Corn Feild & runing thence to the line of ROGER RICHARDSON and Eastward to the land of PETER FFOXON wch. he the sd FFOXON holds for the terme of life, and after to revert to my Son, MOSES, and to his heires as aforesd. And if my Son, MOSES, should die without heires as aforesd that then the land to him given I give & bequeath to my Son, ALEXANDR: as aforesd and to his heires

Item I give & bequeath unto my Son, ALEXANDR: BARROW, all the rest of my land & to his heires of his body lawfully begotten reserving only to my Loveing Wife the Plantation whereon I now live with the houses & orchards thereon contained to her own proper use & behoofe dureing her Naturall life and further it is my will that my Son, ALEXR. shall be at his own disposall in the managemt. of his Estate at Sixteen years of age & to be then possessed of his Estate & if my sd Son should die without heires as aforesd that then I give the land to him given to my Son, MOSES, & to his heires aforesd, & if both my Sons, ALEXANDR. and MOSES, should die without heires as aforesd, that then I give the land given to them to my Son, JONATHAN, & to his heires and further it is my will that if all my three Sons should die without heires of their bodys lawfully begotten that then all my land be devided equally between my two Daughters, HONER & CICELLY BARROW

Item I give unto my two aforesd Daughters one younge mare & one Cow apeice with two pewter dishes one large & one lesser

Item It is my will that the use of my personall estate be equally devided between my loveing Wife, MARY BARROW, & my Son, ALEXANDR:, aforesd suddenly after my decease by my Overseers hereafter named

Item My will & desire is that my debts be paid out of my Debts due to me or other my personall Estate

Item I do make & ordaine my loveing Wife & my Son, ALEXANDER, joynt Executrs. of this my last Will & Testamt. & I do desire my loveing friends, Mr. WILLIAM UNDERWOOD SENR. & Mr. JOHN BURKETT to be my Overseers to take care that this my Will be truely performed, And I also give and bequeath to them my Overseers to each of them a gold ring of Twenty shillings price to be procured by my sd Exectrs. In Witness whereof I have hereunto sett my hand & seale this 3d of Ffebruary 1684

Signed Sealed & made to be his last Will & Testamt.

in presence of us WM. UNDERWOOD SR.   JOHN B BARROW

      JOANE Ŧ UNDERWOOD her marke

      WM. O UNDERWOOD JUNR.

We the underwritten do depose & say that wee did heare Mr. JOHN BARROW say that he did own this within written Will to be his last Will & Testamt: and that wee did see him signe seale & publish it he being then to the best of our Judgmts. in perfect sence

                           WM. UNDERWOOD SENR.

                           WM. UNDERWOOD JUNR.

Proved in Rappa County Court the 6th day of May 1685 by the Oaths of WM. UNDERWOOD SENR. and WM. UNDERWOOD JUNR. and record 19th

pp.
64-
65

IN THE NAME OF GOD Amen. I ROBERT CARDEN of the County of Rappa: being sick of body but of perfect sence & memory do make this my last Will & Testamt. Imprimis: I bequeath my Soul to God and my body to the dust and do dispose of my Temporall Estate in manner & forme following:

Item I give and bequeath my land with all the housing orchards gardens & other appurtinances to my Son, ROBERT CARDEN

Item I will that my Son, ROBERT CARDEN, do after my decease immediately go to live with HUMPHREY DAVIS & his Wife & to continue with them untill he attaine the age of Seventeen years & then to be for himself

Item I will that HUMPHREY DAVIS & his Wife do live in that house now in their possession and enjoy it with what doth belong to it by my fformer agreement with them so longe as they both shall live paying Three hundred pounds of Tobb: and cask p an Rent to my Exectrs.

Item I give unto my Wife, ELIZABETH, all my goods & chattells and my Plantation during her life

Item I will that my Debts be paid by my Exectr.

Item I will ordaine & appoint my loveing Wife, ELIZABETH, Executrx. of this my last Will & Testament & do revoke all former Will or Wills by me had & made & appoint this & none other to be my last Will & Testament. Witness my hand & Seale ffebruary 18th: 1684/5

Signed Sealed & published in the presence of

      THO: PARKER,   ROBERT CARDEN

      WILL: M JONES

Wee underwritten do depose & say that we did heare ROBT: CARDEN say that he did own this within written Will to be his last Will & Testamt. & that we did see him signe seale & publish it he being then to the best of our Judgments in perfect sence & memory & did declare himself so to be   THO: PARKER

                                 WM: M JONES

Proved in Rappa County Court the 6:th day of May 1685 by the Oaths of THOS. PARKER and WM. JONES & record the 19th

p.   IN THE NAME OF GOD Amen, I BRIDGETT RICHARDS being sick of body but of per-
65   fect sence & memory blessed be God do bequeath my body to the grave and my
    Soul to God that gave it mee sure & certaine hopes of Resurrection both sould &
body to endless happiness through the tender mercy of God by the only merits of our
blessed Lord & Saviour Jesus Christ

Item I give unto my foure Children to them & theires all my land to be equally devided
amongst them and this my desire is that my Husband, LEWIS RICHARDS, should have his
lifetime on his new dwelling Plantacon and more over my desire is that Mrs. SISSON
shall keep my Daughter, ANN PRIDHAM, till she is eighteen yeares of age and if she die
before the time is expired for her to give it to whom she will and also my desire is that
Mrs. CALE shall have my Son, CHRISTOPHER PRIDHAM, whilst he comes to the age of
Seventeen years, and if she dieth to dispose of him as she thinks good and will of God be
don. Signed wth: my hand & seale dated the tenth day of Aprill 1685

    MARIA WRIGHT,   BRIDGETT RICHARDS
    THO: + WALKER his mark
    WM. SISSON
Record. xviiii die Maii Ano 1685

pp.   Rappa. County. A Just Accot: of Goods & Estate of ROBERT HENLEY deced as being
65-   sold at an Out-Cry by vertue of an Order of Court bearing date the 4th: of March
66   1684/5

    Imprimis EDWARD JONES with JAMES SANDFORD his security, Confesseth Judg-
mt. for a Cow & Calfe

    Mr. ROBT: CLARKE wth Mr. BARBER his security confesseth Judgment for one
Cow

    EDWARD WETHERBURNE with REUBEN DEALE his security confesseth Judgmt. for
1 cow & a yearling

    HENRY CLARK with WALTER PAVEY security confesseth Judgment for one
Heiffer

    EDWARD WETHERBURNE wth: REUBEN DALE his security confesseth Judgmt. for
two Steeres 4 yeares old

    ROBERT PARK wth: WM: BARBER his security confesseth Judgmt. for one Steare &
a Bull

    Mr. ALEXANDR: SWAN wth: Mr. SAML.: PEACHEY his security confesseth Judgmt.
for one horse

    MORGAN JONES wth: WM. THORNBARY his security confesseth Judgmt: for one
feather bed & boulster a rugg & blanket

    PETER ELDER wth: RICHARD PEACOCK his Security confesseth Judgmt. for one
flock bed & Chaff boulster a rugg & blankett, two pillows, 5 milk trayes, a Skillett & a
Cleaver

    PETER ELLIS with EDWARD JONES his security confessed Judgmt. for a sett of Cur-
tains & Vallens, a Coasting Coat, a high bodied coat & a pare of breeches

    Brought from the other side

    EDWARD JONES wth: JAMES SAMFORD his security confessed Judgmt. for 9 pew-
ter dishes, 2 plates, 9 spoones, 4 Pottangers, 2 tankards, & one bason

    RICHARD DUDLEY wth: EDWARD JONES his security confesseth Judgmt. for a
Chest, Coasting Coat & Looking Glass, & a parcell of Thread & Silk & brass Kettle

    EDWARD WETHERBURN wth: RUBEN DALE his security confesseth Judgmt. in the
behalf of ALEXANDR: DUDLEY for a parcell of Tinnisity

    THOMAS COLLY wth: RODERICK JONES his security confesseth Judgmt. for a
Couch, 2 tables, one pott & pothooks and one beadstead

WM. GLEN wth: RODERICK JONES his security confesseth Judgmt. for one Grind
Stone

PETER ELLIS wth: WM: JONES his security confesseth Judgmt.
wth: security before me   SAMLL. PEACHEY
    Recordr. xix die Maii Ano 1685

pp.   A Parcell of Goods left unsold and valued by us the Subscribers this 30th day of
66-   March 1685
67   3 Course sheets & a shirt Old & torne; 5 Dyapier Napkins & a pr of thred Gloves;
            3 small peices of Needlework lace; 2 Minck Rat skins & 1 Ell of Muslin; 1 new
coal & breeches; 1 old coat & breeches; 1 hatt & one canvas bag, 2 haire sifters, 4 old tin
pans & a frying pan; 1 jarr & an old chest; 2 narrow axes; 2 pottangers & yd. of Kane
Cloth, 1 old chest, 1 two gallon rundlett; 20 lb. of Dried Beefe
                                                    WILL BARBER
                                                    EDWARD JONES
    By 2 old guns without locks; by one Brass Pistoll unfixed; by one gun more   240
                                                    Total 1077

    May the 4th: 1685
    Whereas no Order was granted by the Court for the Appraisemt. of the Estate of ROBT:
HENLEY deced, wee the Subscribers being requested by Mr. RICHARD PEACOCK to value
the same have pformed to the best of our Judgmt. as we are ready to depose
                                                    WM. BARBER
                                                    EDWARD JONES

    Record: xix die Maii Ano 1685

pp.   AN INVENTORY of the Estate of Mr. DOMINICK RICE deced as it was appraised the
67-   18th day of March 1684/5 by us whose names are under written
68   2 old Cows & a bull; 1 very old Horse & one Colt; 1 old Sadle without furniture; 1
            Silver punch cup; 1 broken brass morter & pestell, part of a case of old Knives, 1
old looking glass; 1 old Rapier, 2 suits of old cloaths, 1 old Coasting Coat, 1 old hatt & 1 old
pair of Boots, 5 old Sickles & 3 old Reap hooks, 1 pare old Garden sheeres; 1 Chest without
a key, 1 old Trunck, 5 old leather chaires; 6 old turned chaires; 1 old broken Chaire
table, 100 lb. of old Pewter, 112 lb. of old Iron; 1 old gunn; 2 paire of tongues & a spit; 2
Iron potts & one brass kettle; 1 old warming pan; 2 old broken chests & a broken cub-
bart; 4 old casks, a peice of an old Seaine; 1 old Couch, 1 old Close stoole, 1 pare of small
stilliards; 1 old feather bead & bolster, two ruggs & 2 coverleads, 1 old table & parcell of
Table linen, 1 old Cart & wheeles   Total 4708
                                                    PAUL WOODBRIDGE
                                                    WM. BROCKENBURROUGH
                                                    RICHARD GESPER +
    The sd Appraisers as also Mrs: ANN RICE were sworne before me the 18th of March
1684/5   SAMLL. PEACHEY
    (More one Bill of JOHN MASSEYs)
    Recordr. xix die Maii ano. 1685

p.   March 25th 1685. Then an Inventory of Mr. WEBERs Estate taken and appraised
68   by the Subscribers.
            To one Latine Dixionary & eight other small Latine books, to three sermon
Books bound with Leather of large Quarto & one small old Bible, nine other small books
and a parcell of paper books

To one old Horse of 15 years old; To six yards of black stuff; To an old suit of Cloths & an
old Gownd all torne, To two old pare of Stockings & an old hatt; To two old Shashes all
torne to peices; To two paire of old linen drawers, an old dimity Westcoat & two old Shirts
To a parcell of old Linen as neck cloths & handkerchus & Craps & foure scaines of black
Silk; To an old Saddle & two old Budles & a pare of unfixed pistolls & holsters to them and
an old Sword & two old sadle cloths; To an old Carpet and an old unfixed case of botles, To
a Chamber pott; To one brush; To one Chafing dish & one small Streyner

To one Bill for one Barll: of Corne; more one Bill for a Barll: of Corne; To another Bill
for 247 of Tobb: & cask; another Bill for 2 Bushlls: & halfe of Corne; Some other Bills
wch will be forth coming against the Court by Mrs. RENOLDS

Record: xix die Maii Ano 1685

pp.   June Court 1685
68-   IN THE NAME OF GOD Amen. I NICHOLAS PRITLEE being very sick & weak & likely
69   to depart this World but haveing my perfect senses & remembrance do make this
       my last Will and Testamt. putting by and makeing void all other Wills & Testamts.
by me formerly made. I do bequeath & surrender my Soule unto Almighty God who
gave it me hopeing through his meritorious death to obtaine mercy & forgiveness for
the same through his infinite goodness in his Kingdom of Glory & Immortality. I bequeath my body to its Mother Earth from whence it came there to be buried after a
decent and Christian like manner at and by the discretion of my Wife, MARY PRITLEE,
and for my worldly Estate wch I possess that God hath endowed me wth: both reall &
personall I do dispose of in manner & order following

I do give & bequeath all my Estate both personall & reall unto my beloved Wife, MARY
PRITLEE, for her & her heires forever to have & to hold as my true and lawfull Executrx,
the first paying my debts and Legacies

I do give & bequeath unto one Orphan boy named PETER GANFALLOW a Mare foale to be
delivered to him when he shall come to the age of one & twenty years with her increase
wch: she shall afterwards have

And for the full & some confirmacon & performance hereof I the above named
NICHOLAS PRITLEE have hereunto sett my hand & fixed my seale this Eighteenth day of
Aprill Ano Dom 1685
Signes sealed & delivered in the presence of us

ARTHUR FFORBESS,   NICHOLAS PRITLEE
ROBT. ✠ MILLS
JOHN KING

June 4th 1685 Proved by the Oaths of Mr. ARTER: FFORBESS & ROBT: MILLS in Rappa
County Court then held at Recordt. xxi die

p.   Aprill 3d 1685. In Obedience to an Order of Court to us directed, we the Subscri-
69   bers have valued & appraised what Estate was presented to us by the Widdow &
       Relict of OSWALD JOHNSON deceased in Tobo:
Imprimis One old barren cow; one heifer with her first calfe, more one Cow & calfe,
two yearling; To a sett of Carpenters & Coopers tooles all old; To 2 small pewter dishes; To
3 old pewter dishes & some other old Pewter; To une parcell of old wooden lumber; To
one parcell of old Glass; To a parcell of Nayles; To a small gun; To one old table & forme;
To 1 old Chest; To 1 old Trunk & other old Lumber; To 2 old potts & one old small kettle; To
one parcell of Thred & Shifts for the children; To 3 small remnants of cloath; To one
parcell of old wearing cloths of my Husbands; To one morning gound & petticoat for a
Child; To my wearing cloths; To an old hatt; To one parcell very old lumber; To one bead

& bedstead & all other old furniture   Sum totall 4191

           p   JOHN DANGERFEILD
                ANTHONY NORTH

Sworne before me the 3d of Aprill 1685
     HENRY AWBREY
Recordr. xx die Junii 1685

pp.   AN APPRAISEMENT of the Estate of JAMES ANDREWS deced appraised by us this
69-   19th day of December 1684
70   3 old Coats & a pair of old drawers; 1 paire of old Canvas sheets; 1 old shirt, 1
        old Neck Cloth & a comb case; 4 old books, 2 Horne Combs, 1 old Rugg, an old
Hamock & blankett; 1 old feather bead & coverled, one blankett & pillow; 1 pestell, an old
Sadle, an ax, cutting knife & halter; 21 nayles, a washing tubb & seive; 2 Iron potts, a
hanger, a paire of knit gloves & a paire of yarn stockings, 1 grind stone, 2 Steeres of 4
years old, 4 cowes, 1 heifer 2 years old, and a Bull 3 years old; 2 calves, 5 great shotes, 5
small shotes   Total   5137

   Then above goods appraised by us according to an Order of the Worshpll: Court of the
County of Rappa   ROBT. PLEY
                                  RICHD. GOOD
Sworne before me the day above written   ABRAHAM STAPP
     SAMLL: BLOMFIELD   JOHN SMYTH
   Recordt. xxii die Junii 1685

pp.   July Court 1685
70-   In Obedience to an Order of Court to us directed, we the Subscribers do appraise
71   the Estate of Mr. JOHN BAICON deced as followeth May 20th; 1685
      Item. To a sorrell Mare; two cows, 2 yearlings & a Bull of 2 years old; an old fea-
ther bed & furniture; two Iron potts, 2 Candle Sticks, an old box, an old small box and
chest; a bed, 3 old pillows, 2 old blankets, a Setle bed, six leather chaires, 2 old tables & 3
old chaires, an old Trunk & small case of botles; an old paire of gardin sheeres; 2 old
Swords, a sifter, a cushin, a brush, a looking glass, an old table, a couch, an old Chest, a
spitt, 2 smoothing irons, a parcell of old Tubbs; 2 old flock beds, bolster pillow and an old
rugg; a branding iron, an old Cask, 2 old kettles, a parcell of side cask & powdering Tubb
   It. To a Sider Mill Press; (The Sider Mill to be kept in repaire) & an old pare of Cart
Wheeles & harness, 2 rakes & 2 half tubbs; an old pare of Stilliards, 3 grubbing hoes, a
plow chaine, 2 old ankers, a small cask, an old table cloth & Napkins, To ninety pounds
of pewter

                  Errors Except: ye sum   7635
The appraisers of the above Estate   The Estate appraised by us
were sworne by me   DAVE Ð ƲƤ STARNE
     SAMLL: BLOMFEILD   JOHN Ɉ β BURKETT
   Recordt. xxii die Julii 1685

p.   AN INVENTORY and Apprisemt. of the Estate of JANE KING deced as it was
71   prsented unto us by the Executr: of the sd Estate May 13th 1685
      Item: One feather bed bowlster and stuff to make a paire of Blanketts & rugg, 2
white petty Coats & morning gound damnified; one womans old wast Coat; 2 old aprons,
one lute String hood damnified; one parcell of old head linen; one old apron, an old
paire of bodice & Sleeves; one old Table Cloth & 3 old Napkins, small parcell thread &
Tape, a new stock Lock, one small looking glass, one mugg, one INDIAN baskett & old

razor, one old ax, one old weeding hoe & smll: ditto; one old chest; three old rundletts & old payle, one very old rugg, 2 blanketts & very old catt bed; one old skillet, 2 very old Corne sives; one Meale sive & old baskett; one iron pott & pott hooks, one old tray, a Goard of Salt, one very old tray   11539

   Appraised byus, the above sd

        THO: NEW

        BARNABY mark of ႘ WELLS   The within Appraisers were sworne the day

   Recordt. xxii die Julii 1685   before me   GEO: TAYLER

pp.   IN THE NAME OF GOD Amen. I WILLIAM MOSS SENR. of the County of Rappa-

71- hanock of the Colony of Virginia being at this present very sick and weak in

73   body but of perfect and sound sence & memory blessed by God therefore and considering the uncertainty of mans life in this Mortall world and that all flesh must yeild into death as therefore do make & ordaine this my last Will and Testament in manner & form following (Vizt)

First I give & bequeath my Soul to God that gave it me in sure & certaine hopes of a blessed Resurrection at the last day in and through the meritts death & passion of our Blessed Lord & Saviour Jesus Christ and my body I commit unto the Earth from whence it came to be buried in a decent like sort as by my Exectr. hereafter named shall be thought necessary & convenient

Imprimis After my debts & Legacies are paid, I dispose of that worldly Estate wch. it hath pleased God to bless me wth. as followeth:

Item I give and bequeath unto my Son, WILLIAM MOSS, all this Tract of land and Plantacon whereon I now live conteyning Nine hundred & eighty acres to him and his heires forever; And Six draught Oxen now broak together with Plow & Cart and all materials belonging to them, And I give lunto my sd Son, WILLIAM, one other parcell of land contaying Six hundred acres wch I bought & purchased of JOSEPH CHISELL late of this County deced to him and his heires for ever wth. all writings belonging to the same

Item I do give & bequeath unto my Daughter, FRANCES MOSS, Four hundred acres of land being & adjoyning to the tract of land whereon THOMAS NEWMAN now liveth to her & her heires for ever

Item I do bequeath unto my Daughter, ELIZABETH MOSS, One hundred and fifty acres of land wch I bought of PATRICK NORTON and is adjoyning to the above menconed Six hundred acres of land wch I have given to my Son, WILLIAM, to her & her heires for ever

Item I give and bequeath unto my sd Daughter, ELIZABETH MOSS, Two hundred acres of land whereon THOMAS NEWMAN now liveth, together with the Plantacon and all things belonging to it to her & her heires for ever, & she to enjoy the same as soon as he Leace is out

Item I give & bequeath to each of my Daughters aforesd Two feather beds & furniture belonging to them and each of them one paire of Curtaines and Vallance, one of the beds to be a new one & the other ordinary and I give to my Daughter, ELIZABETH, one great blew rugg and a paire of Cottin blanketts to be for the furniture of her new bed

Item I give & bequeath unto my Daughter, FRANCES, one Cubbard that standeth in the parlour & to my Daughter, ELIZABETH, one small Iron bound Cabbinett and I give each of them my sd two Daughters two Chests & a litle trunk & great one apeice, And I give to my Daughtr: FRANCES, one hoop gold ring that is now in the house and to my Daughter, ELIZABETH, I do give three small silver spoones & one small Dram Cup but not the smallest of all and to my Daughter, FRANCES, I give on Silver Sack Cup. And I do give to my two Daughters aforesd one peice of fine seirge conteyning Twenty seven yards to be equally divided between them & I do give & bequeath unto my Daughter, FRANCES, one black silk gown that was made for her Mother & not more.

Item I give unto my loveing Brother, ROBT: MOSS, one new suit of Cloths to be delivered unto him at my decease that will fitt him; And I give & bequeath unto EDWARD WESTBURY as much of the best Cloth in the house as will make him a Suit of Clothes wth: buttons and Trimming to make it up and that the making be paid for

Item I do give unto THOMAS NEW one Silver Seale wch I had given me by my Sister, CRASK.

Item I do give and bequeath unto my said two Daughters the one halfe of my Pewter both new and old to be equally divided between them and the one halfe of all the Cattle I am possessed of at my decease (Except the Six draught Oxen before given to my Son, WILLIAM) both male & female to be equally divided between them share & share alike to be delivered to them at the day of Marriage or when they come of age which shall first happen; And as for the two or three Remnants of fine Linen it is my Will that my two aforesd Daughters have it to make up for them and I do give unto my Daughter, ELIZABETH, one Negro boy called Docee to her & her heires for ever to be delivered to her at the day of Marriage, and I bequeath to my Daughter, FRANCES, one man Servant to serve the Custome of the Country to be delivered to her at the day of Marriage.

And it is my will & desire that my two aforesd Daughters do continue wth. my Son, WILLIAM, untill they come of age or day of Marriage

Item All other goods merchandizes household stuff & Implements of household stuff, cattle, chatell & all other Estate of what nature kind or Quality soever it be I do give & bequeath unto my Son, WILLIAM, & to his heires forever (Except what is here above given & bequeathed away) only of out of my Stock of Horses I do give & bequeath unto my two abovesd Daughters, FRANCES & ELIZABETH, each of them one horse & one Mare to be delivered to them at the dayes of their respective marriage

Item I do give unto my Daughter, FRANCES, three yewes & a Ram to be delivered to her at the day of Marriage

Item I do give unto my Daughter, ELIZABETH, one heifer & four sheep wch heifer & sheep do go by the name of her Stock and the said heifer & sheep to runn on her Brothers Plantacon untill her marriage day and then to be delivered her together with the female Encrease that shall happen to com to them

Item It is my will and desire further that if either of my abovesd Son & Daughters shall die without issue lawfully begotten of their bodyes that then their reall Estate do fal to the Survivours equaly to be divided

And Finally, I do make & ordaine & appoint my Son, WILLIAM MOSS, abovesaid to be my whole & sole Executr: of this my last Will & Testamt., Revoaking & disannulling all other Wills by me heretofore made or don either by word or writing In Confirmacon whereof I have hereunto sett my hand and affixed my Seale this 21st day of Aprill 1685
Signed Sealed & delivered in the presence of

ROBT. MOSS, ELIAS WILSON,   WILLIAM MOSS
JOHN M MILLS his marke   his mark M

Wee the Subscribers do hereby testifie and declare upon our Oaths that wee did see the within named Testatr: signe seale & deliver this within written to be his last Will & Testamt: and that he was of perfect sence & memory at the signing & sealing hereof to the best of our knowledge   THO: NEW
                                                   JNO. M MILLS

Probatr p Sacrament NEW et MILLS in Cur Com Rappa 1 die July 1685

pp.   Anno 1685 in Virginia
73-   The Estate of Colnll. WILLIAM TRAVERS deced in the hands of Mr. JOHN RICE
77   who married his Adminstrx. vs Debtr.

      To an Inventory of Goods & chattles as p Appraizmt. To a List of Bills & other Debts; To a list of Debts wch: were not Inventoryed; To Tobbo: left in County; To Tobb Reced of Mr. JNO. SAVAGE & JNO. VICKERS in lieu of JAMES KEYs Ball. at 30 lb Sterl. returned reced pt. of 71 lbs. in ye hands of GAW: CORBIN; To the Appraisemt: at EXETER LODGE; To a parcell of goods left unappraised; This par: transacted by SAMLL. GERRARD; To an order of Court against THO: SAMPSON   Total 285861

  To Ballance due from GAW: CORBIN as p sd CORBINs Accot. to Colnll: TRAVERS; 14 hoghdds. of Tobb: shiped to ditto as pr Acct.; Reced of JOSEPH TOWNSEND Debt: of 6 lb. he deducting 300 lb. Tobb: due from Colnll. TRAVERS; Reced of Mr: GEO: SEARL by Ordr. of Court; By goods reced of MATHEW TRAVERSE in part of what he owes   72:09:03

  Memorandum of the Mony debts:

All the Cash in the hands of Mr. MATHEW TRAVERS; Mr. RICE Accot; 72 pounds 12 shil-lings & 7 pence and 12 hogshdd. of Tobb: of wch: no accot. hath been reced tho Mr. RICE had also an order from Capt. FFOX for 91 pounds 1 shilling Mr. GAWIN thinks he ought not to make good till certainly received

  p Contra Credits By funerall charges & other paymts: as p Accot: Currant; By severall paymts. as p Mr: RICE's Accot: By ROWLAND ROWLEYs Bill returned; By JOSEPH COR-NISHes Ditto; By ALEXANDR: NEWMANs ditto; by Sr. HENRY CHICHLEY's ditto; By HEZE-KIAH TRAVERS ditto; by Majr. WHITE's Ditto; by JOB: THOMAS ditto; By WM. WHEELERs ditto; By order against the Estate of THO: PAGE in the hands of VALEN: ALLEN; By WM: MATTHEWS Bill returned; By WM. JOHNSON ditto; By ROBT. HENINGs ditto; By DAVID BURR ditto; by THO: NAYLORs Accot; By GEO: LAMPKINs; By THO: MARSHALL, by GEORGE PEDLERs Bill returned; THO: BROOKES ditto; Mr. BLOMFIELD ditto; JOHN ANSWATH ditto; WILLIAM SHREWSBY ditto; ROBT: SCOTs ditto; JOHN ALLEN ditto; JOHN WORTHs ditto; JOHN RENOLDS ditto; WM. WOOD 3 Bills returned; By Ordr. NORTHUMBERLAND COURT Stoped on SAVINS acct; By Bill of Exchange on Mr. GAWIN CORBIN payable to Mr. SHERWOOD p Order of Court; By one Bill to RALPH WORMLY Esqr.;

  My Ballance of Accot: due: Total 72:00:03

  Lost he haveing absented himself & insolvent, being as per SAMLL. GERRARDs papers of wch: debt lies in ye hands of Mr. GAWIN CORBIN

  CORBIN of LONDON wch: miscarried as Colnll. SPENCER relates so that Mr. RICE pd. for SAMLL. GERARD & my accomodacon at Rablys when (blurred) by KIRTON to TRENT, pd Attorneys fees in sd Business, pd in Ferrys in going & coming from TOWN, Brought in Ballance by GEORGE JONES in full of 700 Tobb: spent by Colnll. TRAVERS his house; pd the Sheriff of NORTHUMBERLAND in KIRTONs Business; By Attorney's fees, 3 Ferryes over NOMANY going & coming for to abate 2400 lb. Tobb: charged by sd KERTON for charges; ffor goods bought by my Wife of Mr. KEYZER wch was by mistake appraised in the Estate; pd Sheriffs fees to Mr. CARTY & Mr. ROBERTS the year 79; pd Clerks fees more than formerly charged to Capt. CRASK, pd Clerks fees in LANCASTER COURT as Acct: till Novembr: 79; pd Clerk Sheriff & attorneys fees not recovered since 79; pd 5 hoghdd. of Tobb: that were Rotten at RICHD. WOODs & else where; Charges of recovering Mr. CRAIDONs Bill of 692, 1 of MAX ROBINSON, SIMM GRAYes Note to WM. YOUNG neither note not reced; Due to JOHN SHURLOCK neither not not received; Ballance of HENRY STONHAM as pr SAMLL. GERARD as RABLEYes upon SHERWOODs action against the Estate not charged till now; Sallary of Receiving 122017 lbs. Tobb: at 10 plntt. For the balance of COTHERNs Debt not finding Bill nor reced; deduct out of the above acct: per Order of Court   22797

In Performance of an Order of this Worshipll: Court we the Subscribers haveing examined the above menconed account and made inspection on the severall particulars
thereof exhibited to ous by Mr. JOHN RICE dated this 16th day of June 1685

> SAMLL. PEACHEY
> ALEXANDR: SWAN
> JNO. BAYLEY
> JOHN SAMPSON

A list of the Debts paid by Mr. JOHN RICE:
To pay Lt: Colnll. WM. LOYD as Attorney of Mr. JOHN SAVIN inpart of an Order of Court
for 8000 or thereabouts; To pd Colnll. XPHR. WORMLEY by ordr. of Court; To pd Capt.
CRASK, JOSIAS DRAPER; for 1 cow at the LODGE to SAMLL. TRAVERS appraised into the
Estate & returned to him; Discounted p HEZECHIA COLLIDGE p Colnll. TRAVERS note; By
THO: KIRTONs 2 Bills charged in the Inveotyr & returned him by Court to sd KIRTON by
ordr. of WESTMORELAND COURT; Discount by FRANCIS ELMORE out of his Bill for 2000 for
work done for Colnll. TRAVERS; pd WM. SMYTH by order of Court; Mr. JOHN TAVERNER
his fee in or; concerne against SMYTH of DUBLIN; pd RICHD: BRAY for Colnll. TRAVERS
Bill to Mr. FRANCIS TOMPSON; pd Mr. GOLDMAN by Ordr. of Court; Colnll. SPENCER; Mr.
HONSSING; by ROBT: EDGHILL as p SAMLL. GERARDs Acct. Ballance of HENRY CHAPLE for
Mr. WETHER Bill not reced; Bal. of ALEXR. ENGLISH acct. by SAMLL. GERRARD over
charged in the list of Debts not entered in the Inventory as over paid Capt. FPOWLES
2160 wch should be but 2116; over charge in Two Bills of HEZICHIA TURNERs

> Rappa County Court July 2d 1685

This Court doe find that the Estate of Colnll. WM. TRAVERS according to the above and
within Accot: is Indebted to the Relict & Orphans of the sd Colnll. TRAVERS in Tobb
137331 1 Tobb: And in money as by the proceeding Account

> Test WM. COLSTON, Cl Cur

Recordr. xxiii die Julii Ano Dom 1685

p.   August 1685
77   AN INVENTORY of the Estate of RICHD. ELLITT deced taken & appraised this 18th
        of June 1685

Imp. 1 Cow & calfe; 1 steere 2 years & 1 heyfer; 1 chest, old wth: out a lock; 2 small pots
& 1 paire of pothooks; 1 old Musquett, 1 old fry pan & 4 hooks; a parcell of old Carpenters tooles & old iron; an old cross cut Saw & old wedges; 2 Rundells, 1 butter pott, 1 paile
3 milk trayes, 1 old Salt box; 1 old bed Stead; 1 pestle & old Couch broken; 2 old mele seves
1 carpenters adds, 1 old Chisell & cold punch   1436

> Appraised by us   JOHN CATLETT
>   JOHN POWELL

Record xxiii die Augst. 1685

pp.   A TRUE INVENTORY of JOHN ERWINs Estate appraised by FRANCIS STONE &
77-   DAVID STERNE & sworne to by Mr. HARRIS May the 26th: 1685 according to Order
78   of Court

2 Cows & Calves, one Cow & one Heifer, one gelding, sadle & 2 bridles; one
barrow & one Sow, 2 yews & one lamb; one sett of Coopers tooles, 2 Sider Butts & one
forty Gall. Cask; one sett of Shirt buttons & one Tobb: box; 2 Ivory hafted knives; a small
parcell of Browne thread; one paire of Spurs; one horne Comb & tobb: box; one pare of
Worsted hose & one pair yarne ditto; two new Muzlin Neckcloths; 2 old holland Neckcloths & 2 old Handkerchus, 2 old Dowlas shirts, one paire of old lether drawers &
leathr: apron, one very old serge suit, 3 old blue shirts, one new serge suit lyned, one

serge suit unlyned & woare, one Dimity suite new, one cloth coat very old, 6 yards of
Course Seirge, one Bill of RICHARD DRAKEs, a pare old French falls, one broad hoe, one
Gun, one shott bagg & powder horne & belt; one parcell of shott, one horse whip, one
chest   The sum in all is   6804
  The Appraisers sworne before me
        JAMES HARRISON
  Recordr. xxii die Sept 1685

p.   AN ACCOT: of the Estate of DOMINICK RICE deced 1685 delivered & Exhibited by AN
78   RICE his Administrx.
        By the Inventory; to what is pd. over paid; By Mr. ROBT. CLARK for meanes my
last sickness of Mr. DOM RICE p Judgmt; by 1 hdd. of Tobb & three pr Judgmt; By ordr. of
Court payable to JNO. BEARE for Wheat; By Clerks fees; by funerall charges; p Order of
Court; By appraisers Accot; By Attorneys fees in defence of severall actions;   5214
  Wee the Subscribers being appointed by the Worshipll. Court of Rappa. to examine this
Accot: finde it proved according to wt; is cast up but the Attorneys fees we leave to yor:
. Worships Judgments.
                                        JNO. BAYLEY
                                        WM. MOSELEY

  Errors Excepted ANN $\bigwedge \mathbb{R}$ RICE
   Record xxii die Sept: 1685

p.   A JUST ACCOUNT of what SAMLL. WHITHEAD deced possessed of & taken this 17th
79   of August 1685
        Imprimis: WM. BARBER by Bill & Acct; THO: DUE p Accot: THO: COLLEY by Bill;
  WM. LOYD p Accot: JNO. POWELL p Accot; PAULL WOODBRIDGE, JOHN BAYLIS, Mr. WM.
FANTLEROY, RUBEN DALE, Mr. ALEXANDR: SWAN; ANDW: DUE; RICHD. JESPER; JERE-
MIAH PHILLIPS, ROBT. CLARK, THO: COLLEY, XPHER THOMAS,   . ANN RICE p Bill;
11214. THOMAS CHITTY Debtr. p Acct: Money accts; more Tobb. Accr. Mr. GEORGE Acct;
JNO. INGOE p Accot: 12219
  Recordatr. xxi die Sept: 1685

pp.   Rappa. County. AN INVENTORY of the Estate belonging to Capt. JOHN ROLT de-
78-   ceased appraised by Mr. HENRY HACKENREE and Mr. JOHN OWENS, Sworne by
80   Mr. ANTHONY SAVAGE this 9th day of July 1685 as followeth:
        To one old feather bed & bolster, one Cow & Calfe & a yearling heiffer; two old
Brass kettles & one old iron pott & some old dishes & a plate; fire tongs & fire shovell;
two spitts & a paire of old doggs, a fire pann & a paire of pott racks; to a flesh fork, a
ladle and grid iron; 2 old chests, one old warming pan & one old drippin pan; one old
cross cut saw & an old hand saw; an old grubbing hoe
  All things being compleated that the Order of court requires
                                HENRY ┼┼ HACKER
                                JOHN ┼O OWENS
  The Widow gave in the last Inventory 2 cows and heifer not belonging to the Estate of
her Husband being ignorant of those affaires & to the prooff I can make it appeare by
Oath I do desire of the Worshipll. bench to be allowed of my Husbands Estate these
charges as followeth: To the Doctr. for visits & meanes on his death bed; To his Coffin,
To his funerall   950
  Recordr. Cur Com Rappa xxi die Sept. 1685

pp.   IN THE NAME OF GOD Amen this fiftyfifth day of October in the yeare of our Lord
80-   One thousand Six hundred Eighty & foure I JAMES COGHILL of Sittenburne
81   Parish in Rappa County, Plantr., in health in body & in perfect minde &
        memory thanks be given unto God therefore calling into minde the Mortality of
my body and knowing that it is appointed for all men once to die do make and ordaine
this my last Will & Testament in manner & forme following that is to say, first & principally I give my Soul into the hands of God who gave it me & for my body I commend it
to the Earth to be buried in Christian & decent manner, nothing doubting but at the
Generall Resurrection I shall receive the same againe by the mighty Power of God.
  And as touching such worldly Estate as it hath pleased God to bless me with in this life
I give devise bequeath & dispose the same in manner & forme following
  Ffirst I give & bequeath unto my loveing Wife, MARY COGHILL, the Plantacon whereon I live during her life with all my house hold goods & all my hoggs & Catle, one Mare
& one horse & if she dies a Widdow then to be divided amongst all my Children and next
  I bequeath to my Eldest Son Two hundred Twenty five acres of land with one Mare with
all Coopers & Carpentrs. tooles to be equally divided between WILLIAM & JAMES
  Next I bequeath to my Son, JAMES, Two hundred twenty five acres of land, one Mare &
my own Gun & sword and next bequeath to my Son, DAVID, two hundred acres of land
and one mare & one Gun & next I bequeath to my Son, FREDERICK, Two hundred acres of
land; To a Child unborne if a boy I bequeath Two hundred acres of land, if not to return
to four above menconed
  And to my Son, FREDERICK I bequeath one Mare.
  All wch land given of one dividend to be equally divided according to Quantity & Quality every one takeing their portions as they are capable to manage it; every one according to age to take their choice
  Now I bequeath to my Daughters, MARGRETT & MARY, Six hundred acres of land lying
in another Dividend, Two hundred acres of this land to a Child unborne if a girle if not
to remaine to the above MARGRETT & MARY; And the increase of DAVID & FREDERICK
Mares to return to MARGRETT & MARY each of them one Mare of a yearl old aforesaid.
  I do appoint DAVID & FREDERICK to be at age at Eighteen & to enjoy their Estate if their
Mother marryeth.
  I make & ordaine my well beloved Son & my loveing Wife my full and sole Executr. &
sole Executrx. ratifieing & confirming this & none other to be my last Will and Testa-
ment.
  In Witness whereof I have hereunto sett my hand & seale the day & yeare first above
written
Signed sealed & published & delivered
by the sd JAMES COGHILL to be his last
Will & Testament
        CHRISTOPHR: ⊘ MAN,   JAMES COGHILL
        THOMAS ⋜ FENLEY
Rappa Court Sept. 1685. Wee the Subscribers doe depose & say that the within Testatr:
did signe seale & publish the within Will as his last Will & Testament & that the sd Testatr. was at the time of his signing & sealing the same of perfect sence & meory to the
best of yor: Deponents knowledge & further say not
                                        THOMAS ⊘ FENLEY
                                        CHRISTOPHR: 𝓜 MAN

  Proved in Rappa County Court the first day of Septembr: 1685 by the Oaths of FENLY &
MAN. Recorded the 21st of the sd Month

p.   Novembr: 1685. IN THE NAME OF GOD Amen. I CORNELIUS REYNOLDS in the
81   Freshes of Rappahannock being sick & weak in body but in perfect sence &
        memory praised be to God for it. Imprimis I commend my Soule to God almighty
& my body to the grave to be decently buried

Item I make & appoint my loveing & kind Wife, MARGERY REYNOLDS, my whole & sole
Executrx. of all & every parcell of my Estate and all moveables only the Seat of Land
where I now live to be divided equally either of them to have Plantacon, my Son, WIL-
LIAM REYNOLDS, to have the choice & JOHN REYNOLDS the other halfe with one Plantacon

Item I give unto my Grandson GOSS the first mare foal to him with her increase for
ever. This is my whole & sole Will & Testamt. Revokeing all other Wills & Testamts. As
Witness where I have put my hand & seale this 29th day of September 1684.
Signed Sealed in the presence of us
        THOMAS HOOP his marke ☩   COR: REYNOLDS
        MARY HOPE; MATT: @ LASRY
Wee the Subscribers do depose & say that wee saw the within named Testatr: signe
seale & publish this within as his last Will & Testamt. & that at the time of signing &
sealing of the same he was of perfect sence & memory to the best of yor; Depts: knowledge & further say not   THOMAS ☩ HOPE
                                                        MARY ✓ HOPE

Proved by the Oaths of THOMAS & MARY HOPE the 4th; day of Novembr: 1685 before
Colnll. JOHN STONE, Capt. GEO: TAYLER & Capt. SAMLL. BLOMFIELD and recorded the 17th
of the sd month

                    Teste WM. COLSTON Cl Cur Com Rap:

pp.   Novemb: 25th 1685
81-   IN THE NAME OF GOD Amen. I JOHN SAMPSON at the prsent in the County of
84   Rappa: in Virginia, Mercht., being of sound mind & memory praised be God, do
        make and declare my last Will & Testamt. as followeth; first & principally I do
hereby recommend my Soul into the hands of the Almighty who gave it me & my body I
commit to the Earth to be decently buried as herein expressed, Trusting it shall partake
of that Glorious Resurrection purchased by the Redeemer of the World Christ Jesus but
my desire is no sermon be preached at my funerall, my body to be put into a decent
coffin & carryed to the grave by Six Merchants if they may be had otherwise by six of
the Commission of this County And desire that there be no more than three gallons of
Strong Liquor (without Victualls) be therefore expended; And as for that worldly Estate
God of his goodness hath blessed me with I dispose thereof as is herein exprest

 Imprimis. My mourning Ring I give & bequeath to my Loveing Sister, REBECCA
SAMPSON

 I give & bequeath unto Mrs. SARAH SUGGITT my little Bible with Silver Clasps, my Silver Spoone, my Silver Punch Cup, my Book in folio written by HEINE and Two other
books I Heavin Opened by R:A: the other the Life & Death of Mr. JOHN JANIWAY

 I give & bequeath unto my loveing Brothers, JACOB & ISACK SAMPSON, Thirty Shillings
to buy each of them morning Rings wch: sd Rings & money or Tobb: the value of the sd
Mony to be sent by some Trusty friend to the use aforesd (Vizt.) My mourning Ring to
my Sister & the Thirty Shillings to my Brothers, my Silver Seale likewise I give unto my
Brother, JACOB

 I give unto my loveing friend, Mr. JOHN TAVERNER, my Books entitled "Religio
Modica" and the French Accademy

 My desire & my express meaning is that what Toba: of mine can be had & at any time

need may be consigned to my honored ffather Mr. PTOLOMIOUS SAMPSON of Tattons to
whom I give & bequeath the same; And as for my wearing appareell and all other
things of mine not before disposed of my desire is that it may be sold all at an Out Cry &
when my debts are paid to consigne the overplus to my Father; But in case of his decease before such Consignment: shall be made I desire the same may be consigned to
my loveing Brother, ISACK SAMPSON in LONDON to the use of himself, my loveing Brother JACOB & my loveing Sister, REBECCA (Vizt. one half to my sd two Brothers ISACK &
JACOB & the other half to my said Sister, REBECCA).

   My minde & will further is that all my Books of Acct. remain in the house of Mr. JOHN
SUGGETT whom I make & ordaine full & sole Executr. to this my prsent & last Will & Testamt. to see the same performed as far as in him shall lye & when the business of my
Estate shall be finished I desire him to consigne the said Books of Account to my
honored Father, if he be deceased, then to either of my Brothers, and I do hereby
revoke all former Wills by me made or spoake & ordaine this & no other to stand as my
last Will & Testament In Witness whereof I have hereunto sett my hand & seale this
seventh day of Septembr: 1684

   I desire my body may be buried at Mr. JOHN   JOHN SAMPSON
SUGGETTs being the first house I lived at in
these parts
Signed Sealed and delivered in the presence of (blank)
Probatr p Circumstans in Cur Com Rappa 25 die 9bris 1685

   Inventorie of what Goods belong to Mr. JOHN SAMPSON deced at the house of Mr. WIL-
LIAM SLAUGHTER this 10th day of Novembr: 1685 by us whose names are hereunto
subscribed being thereto requested by Mr. SAMLL. PEACHEY & are still remayning in
Custody of Mr. SLAUGHTER
   Imprs. In a large trunk one Course Towell, one ditto Pillober; 4 pare of Sleeves, 4 caps,
2 hand kercheis, 2 neck cloths, one shirt; 1 paire of drawers, a sea rugg, 1 feather pillow, one pair of old Worsted Stockings, 1 old feltt; 1 stuff suit; one dimity suit, 1 new
black serge suit, 1 pillow beer, one old neck cloth, & small leather bagg; 1/2 lb. of
whited coruse Thread; 34 skeines of Calamid & Bro: thread; coloured & bro: thread; 1/2 a
gross of black Silk buttons, Sixty yards of filliting, 2 yds. of fenetting, 1 pare of black
worstead stockings; 6 pr of small wrist cuffs, 1 shoulder knott
                         In a Chest
   Two pares of fall shooes, 5 doz of Cloak buttons, one small looking glass, 1 razors &
cases; a womans spangled head Roal, a small box wafers, one brush, a small angling
line, one large earten pott, a Cane, a Whip, boos, Viz: "The Heart kept from Dissinding",
Religio Medice" "A Seamans Calender of Friendship" & of a friend MICHLL. COPE of the
Provers "Heaven Opened" p R. A. a French Grammar "Poore man familie book p BAXTER,
POWELLs Concordance, one Bridle & sadle, a small trunk of writeings sealed wth: the sd
SAMPSONs owne Seale; the Frame to a Latch, 3 turning Chissells, 3 D. Gouges & 3 plaines
                         JOHN RICE
                         ALEXR. SWAN
                         JNO. BAYLEY

Recordr. 5 die 10bris 1685

   A particular of what Goods was found in Mr. JOHN SAMPSONs Store the next day after
his Burriall being the 9th day of Novembr: 1685 by us whose names are hereunto subscribed & are as followeth Vizt.:
   IN THE GREAT CHEST. Six paire of ffalls & 7 of plaine shooes & budle headstall &

Raignes two other pare of plaine shooes 5000 Pinns 1 gross & halfe of Mettle buttons 5 knives with sheaths & one old knife without, 8 paire of small & three paire of bigger Scissers, 4 doz. of thread laces, 2 pieces of Nanock Tape, 2 pounds of Brown thread, a case of ffleames, 4 small papers of whtied browne thread; 2 Ivory small combs about an ounce as may be left of Sticking Silk, 22 yards of Galvinne; 11 yards of Kersey, No. 10; one yard a half & half Quarter of Broad cloth; 10 yards 3 qts of half thick Kersey

IN THE LESSER CHEST Two bed tickings, a whip comb, bridle 7 lb of Browne thread half a dozen of Pewter Spoones, one pound of Coloured thread; one pound & halfe of Browne thread half a gross of white wast coat buttons half a gross of Coat silk buttons, 2 hanks & a peice of coloured Silk, a pare of scissers, 5 small hatt Rubbers, Law books of this country; a Bible wth. Silver clasps, a Book of FRAN: QUARLES intitled "Dinne Fancys" another of JOHN QUARLES, two gun belts, one small & the other great one hilling hoe & a weeding hoe about a pound of Gun powdr: in a small barrell 33 1 of Goose shott, a cask of Salt, cont: 84 gallons as is get at; 1 barrell of three bushells and the other about 4 a half bushell & a Neck measure

IN THE LOFT 23 felt hatts; 13 hilling hoes & a grubbing hoe; 18 hat bands, 2 handles for a Syth wth: wedges & Iron, Ginger madeale box 18 pounds weight, a small joyners plane, of Nayles 6, 8, 10, 27 lbs. in weight together 1700 Tobb. nayles, a Rum puncheon wherein is 13 inches or thearabouts in depth of Rum; a Cask of Sugar we are Informed when full held 460 lb. & now not about a 3rd full; a small Silver Punch cup, a pewter pint pott, a flock bed boulster claimed to be bought by RALPH DOWNING at 900 lb: Tobb: not yet paid for. A bed Sted

| JOHN RICE | ALEXR: SWAN |
| JNO. BAYLY | JO: TAVERNER |

The day & yeare above written, Mr. JOHN SUGGETT did ingage to take the above menconed particulars into his Charge & Custody wch: was so thought necessary he desiring the same by reason there was a Will found amongst Mr. SAMPSONs papers wrott all wth. his own hand wherein he was nominated sole Execut. In Wittness whereof the sd JOHN SUGGETT doth hereby oblige himself for the Receipt of the said particulars by his hand sett hereunto

Test   JOHN RICE   JAMES SUGGETT
               ALEXR: SWAN
               JNO. BAYLY

Recordatr Cur Com Rappa 7 die Decembr: 1685

pp.   10br 21st 1685
84-   IN THE NAME OF GOD Amen. I HONORIA JONES, Widdow & Relict of Mr. GEORGE
85   JONES being sick & weak of body but of perfect sence & memory blessed be God
          do make my last Will & Testamt. in manner & forme following

First I bequeath my Soule to God that gave it and my body to the Earth to be decently buried at the discretion of my Surviveing friends hoping for a joyfull Resurrection of the same in & through ye meritts of our blessed Lord & Saviour Jesus Christ And as to the portion of worldly goods wch. it hath pleased God to endow me withall I do give & dispose as followeth

Secondly, I give & bequeath unto my Daughter, MARGRETT BLAGG, that Seat or Tract of land wch I purchased of Colnll. JOHN VASSALL lying & being on the South side of Rappa River contaying Eleven hundred seventy & five acres the sd land to be at her absolute sole disposall for ever

Thirdly, I give & bequeath unto my Daughter, ELIZABETH GARDNER, my Wedding Ring wch joyned me and my Husband, Majr. JOHN WEIRE in Matrimonie

4thly. I give unto my Son in Law, Mr. ABRAHAM BLAGG, twenty Shillings to buy him a mourning Ring

5thly. I give unto my Son, Mr. RICHARD GARDNER, a Knife, a Ring of the aforesd value

6thly I give unto my Grandchild, RICHARD WATTS, one Silver Spoone, one Silver Truncher Salt

7thly I give unto my Grandson, EDWARD BLAGG, the same aforesd

8thly I give unto my Grandon, ABRAHAM BLAGG, the like

9thly I give unto my Grandon, LUKE GARDNER, the same

10thly I give unto my Grandson, JNO. GARDNER the same

Lastly, I do hereby constitute ordaine & constitute my well beloved Daughter, MARGRETT BLAGG, Wife of Mr. ABRAHAM BLAGG, to be my sole Executrix of this my last Will and Testamt. revoking all other Wills & Testamts. by me heretofore made And hereunto have interchangably sett my hand & seal this 9th day of Novem: 1685
Signed Sealed & delivered in the presence of us

    JAMES HARRISON,   HONORIA JONES
    ANDW. A-CONEBY,
    MICHAELL BASSEY

I the Subscriber do depose & say that I did see the within named Mrs. HONORIA JONES signe seale & deliver this within written as hir last Will & Testamt. & that she was then in perfect sence & memory at the signing & sealing thereof
Sworne to before us the 16th day of Decemr: 1685

    HENRY AWBREY   MICHAELL ✝ BASSEY
    GEO: TAYLER   his mark

I the Subscriber do depose & say that I saw the within named Testatrx. signe seale & deliver this within written as hir last Will & Testament and that she was of perfect sence & memory at the time of signing & sealing the same & further saith not
                             JAMES HARRISON

Probatr in Cur Com Rappa 21 die Decembris 1685 et Recordatr 4 die January

pp.   JOHN JENNINGS Part:
85-   To one ffeather bed, one boulster, two pillows, 2 straw pads, one pare of sheets,
87   one blanket, one worsted rugg, one sett of curtaines, one bedstead, two old
          pewter basons, one pewter dish large, two hoes, two reap hooks, one driping pan
one Bible, one Sermon book, one table & forme, two wooden chaires, one looking glass, one warming pan, one Iron pott, two brass candlesticks, one old Gun, one spade, one spitt, one chest, three wedges Iron

    WILLIAM JENNINGS Part:
One feather bed & one worsted rugg, one boulster & two pillowes & one pare of sheets, one blankett, one sett of Curtaines & one beadstead; two old pewter basons, one old pewter dish, three plates & salt, 2 hoes, two reap hooks, one dripping pail, one Bible & Sermon Book, one table & one form, 3 wooden chaires, one small brass kettle, one small iron pott, one auger & trowell, one claw hammer & paire of sheep sheres, two pewter spoones, one Gun & Pitch fork, two frying pans, one chest, three barrow of three years old; three barrows of two years old, one breding sow, 4 cows & calves

    CHRISTOPHER EDRINGTONs Part
To two feather beds old, two blanketts, two ruggs, three sheets, two bedsteads, two boulsters, one old pewter bason, one small pewter dish, one old pewter dish, three plates, one old pewter tankard, three pewter spoones, two hoes, two reap hooks, one driping pan, one Bible, one Sermon Book, one small Table, one chess press, one spining wheele & cards, one large brass kettle, one pare of large fire tongs, one pare of pott hooks, one tin chafin dish, one tin pudding pan, one iron pestell & broad ax, one cross

cut saw, one pare of Pincers, two old Chissells, one barrell of a gun, one Chest, 3 Barrows of 3 yeares old, 3 barrows of 2 yeares old, one breeding Sow,
Wee the Subscribers have equally divided the Estate according to Will as witness our hands   FRANCIS STONE
                                                         GILES MATHEWS

Recordatr. Cur Com Rappa 4 die Janry 1685

pp.   February Court 1685/6
87-   IN THE NAME OF GOD Amen. I GEORGE BOYCES of County of Rappa being sick &
88   weake of body yet of perfect sence & memory do make this my last Will & Testa-
        mt. in manner & forme as followeth. Imprimis I bequeath my Soule to God that
gave it & my body to the Dust in hopes of Resurrection to Life at the last day through
Jesus Christ our Lord & Saviour & do dispose of my Temporall Estate as is here Expressed
   Item I give and bequeath unto Mr. JOHN DANGERFIELD Two hundred & fifty acres of
land of that tract of land called the RANGE LAND to him & his heires forever the sd Two
hundred & fifty acres of land to be on that side of the sd tract next to the land that
BRYAN WARD now liveth on
   Item I give & bequeath unto JEREMIAH PARKER Two hundred & fifty acres of land of
the same tract called ye: RANGE & joyning to the abovesd 250 bequeathed to Mr. JOHN
DANGERFIELD to him the sd JEREMIAH PARKER, Son of THO: PARKER, to have hold &
enjoy to his heires forever
   Item I give & bequeath the residue of the abovesd tract of land called ye RANGE all
whole & singular with the appurtenances (saving & excepting what is above
bequeathed) unto my loveing Sister, DOROTHY BOYCES als BROWNE to have hold & enjoy
the sd tract of land called the RANGE (saving what is above excepted) to her the said
DOROTHY BOYCES als BROWNE & to her heires for ever
   Item I give & bequeath unto my God Daughter, SARAH SHIPLEY, Daughter of DANLL:
SHIPLEY, Two hundred and fifty acres of land that I hold by Patent & conveyance lying
in this County of Rappa on the South side of the River in the Parish of South Farnham &
joyning to the land of Mr: JOSEPH GOODRICH & to the land of THOMAS WOOD to have hold
& enjoy the sd 250 acres of land with the appurtinances to her the sd SARAH SHIPLEY &
her heires for ever
   Item I give & bequeath unto FRANCES DANGERFIELD, Daughter of Mr. JOHN DANGER-
FIELD, one gold ring with 3 barrs and a Stone in it being the least of three stone rings
that I have
   Item I will that my horses & Mares & what Debts is due unto me be to pay my Debts
withall and the residue of my personall Estate after my Debts are paid I give & bequeath
unto my beloved Sister, DOROTHY BOYCES als BROWNE
   Item I will & ordaine & appoint my beloved Sister, DOROTHY BOYCES als BROWNE
Executrx. of this my last Will & Testamt. joyning wth her as overseer & assistant Mr:
JOHN DANGERFIELD & I will that what Tobb: is of mine in the hands of Mr. JOHN
DANGERFIELD be by him expended disburst in the paying of my Sisters passage into this
Country
   Item I will that my man, GRACE, be & remaine wth: Mr. JOHN DANGERFIELD untill my
Sister comes in to this Country unless he can dispose of him on a good Acct: towards the
defraying of charges either of my Sisters passage or other charges that he may be at in
manageing my Estate in whose hands (to wit) Mr: JOHN DANGERFIELDs, I will that my
Estate may remaine untill my Sister doth arive in Virginia
   Item I give revoak and make null & void all former Wills by me had & made & do
appoint this & no other to be my last Will & Testament willing & requesting Mr: JOHN

DANGERFIELD to see that my funerall be solemnized decently at the house where I die & that a funerall Sermon be preached for me at the LOWER CHURCH of Scittenburne Parish by the first opertunity of a Minister

Item that if in case my Sister, DOROTHY, should not come into the County, my will is that my land that is not already above bequeathed (to witt) the residue of that tract of land caled the RANGE be disposed of and I do dispose of it thus Viz: I give unto Mr: JOHN DANGERFIELD Children Eight hundred acres of land residue like to be equally divided between them and to THOMAS PARKERs Children Eight hundred acres of the sd land to be equally divided between them and to DANLL. SHIPLEYs Children, Nine hundred acres of the sd land to be equally divided between them, there being three thousand acres in the whole In consideracon of all these above recited premises & In Testimony that this is my last Will and Testamt. I hereunto sett my hand & seale this eight day of January 1685/6

Signed Sealed & Published in the presence of
> THO: PARKER,   GEORGE BOYCES
> DANLL. Ø SHIPLEY,
> ALICE Ø SHIPLEY

Wee whose names are here underneath subscribed do depose & say that in our Sight & hearing GEO: BOYCES did signe seale and publish this within Will as his last Will and Testamt.
>   THO: PARKER
>   DANLL. Ø SHIPLEY
>   ALICE Ø SHIPLEY

Proved in the County Court of Rappa: by the oaths of THO: PARKER, DANLL. SHIPLEY & ALICE SHIPLEY the 3 day of February 1685/6 and record the 9th die of the sd month & yeare

p.   THE INVENTORY of what goods belonged to RICHARD DAVIS who lately deceased
88   at the house of RALPH WHITLOW and vallued by us WILLIAM COVINGTON &
      DANLL. DOBYNS

Imprs. A horse bridle saddle & cloth; his wearing cloths, a Cutlas & belt, his carpenter tooles   1620

>   Test   DANLL. DOBYNS
>   WILLIAM Λ COVINGTON
Janry. the 11th 1685/6 Recordr. Cur Com Rappa 9 die ffeb. 1685/6

p.   January the 30th 1685/6 AN INVENTORY of the Estate of WALTER LODOWICK
88   taken & appraised by us the Subscribers
      Imprs. To one heifer 3 years old, 2 heyfers 4 years old each; one cow, one 2 yeare old Bull; one parcell of Carpenters tooles, an old hatt & old paile, To one suit cloths
>   JOHN P GOUGE
>   HEN: I H JORDAN

Sworne before me this 1st day of Febry 85
>   HEN: AWBREY
Recordt. 9 die ffeb: 1685/6

pp.   INVENTORY of the Estate of Mr. CORNELIUS REYNOLDS deced
88-   Imprimis: 2 tables, 4000 l of Tobb: being the crop wch: was made on the Planta-
90   con by the people belonging to the Estate; 3 old Cows & 1 Calfe, 3 cows, 2 heyfers
      & a young steere; 3 calves 2 yeares old, one old mare & one old horse & one colt; 2 feather beds & furniture & 3 Serge curtaines wth: silk fringe; a paire of white curtains,

60 lb of pewter being very old, one pewter flaggon, parcell of old Brass, one dozen of old Chaires; one silk mantle being laced round wth: Silver lace; one old chest of drawers; 6 ole chests without Locks & some of them without hinges & one old trunk, a parcell of lumber Vizt. old Barrells & Trayes; 2 pestles, a paire of andirons, 3 pot racks, 2 old spitts, 2 potts & pothooks the iron potts haveing holes in them, a sett of wedges, one broken carbine & some old iron tooles, a harness for 2 horses & two old sadles, 2 Servants old beds & covering; a parcell of old table linen; some old books, a pare of old stilliards; 2 old casks & two old cases, one Servant man haveing one crop to make; To 5350 Tobb: wch: were debts due the sd Estate & are now received, a leading Staff
        20360

Mrs. MARGERY REYNOLDS made oath that this is a true inventory of her deced Husband Mr. CORNELIUS REYNOLDS Estate which is Twenty thousand Three hundred & sixty pounds of Tobb   ANTHONY SAVAGE
    There is omitted in the Inventory one old Spade & one pale and one old Couch
    Recordr. Cur Com Rappa 9 die February 1685/6

    Account of Tobacco paid p Mrs: MARGERY REYNOLDS, Executrx. of the Last Will & Testament of her Husband, Mr; CORNELIUS REYNOLDS deced:
    Imprimis To Tobb. paid the Honble Colnll. NICHOLAS SPENCER; paid Mr. NICHOLAS WEARE, Colnll. JONES on the Acct. of Mr. DUNBAR; paid EDMOND GEORGE, pd for Leveys; pd Colnll. JONES on the acct. of SEABRIGHT; pd Mr. EDWARD THOMAS on the acct. of SEABRIGHT; pd Colnll: FITZHUGH; pd JOSEPH BECKLEY, pd SIMON TOMAZIN, Capt. COOPER, Mr. MOORE; To 1050 lb. of Tobb: wch: must be taken out of the Estate of Mr. CORNELIUS REYNOLDS deced and belonging to the Orphans of Capt. THOMAS WILLIAMS
    Oath made before me to the Payment of the here specifyed
                                                    ANTHONY SAVAGE

    Recordt. 9 die February 1685/6

p.   IN THE NAME OF GOD Amen. I JAMES YEATS being sick & weak but of sound &
90   pfect memory (praised be God for it) doe ordaine this my last Will & Testamt. in
        manner & forme following:
    Imprimis I bequeath my Soule into the hands of Almighty God my Savir: & Redeemer trusting in & through him that my Soule may receive everlasting Salvation & my body to be decently buried by my Exectrs. hereafter named
    Item I doe ordaine my well beloved friend, WILLIAM CLAPHAM, my whole & sole Exectr. of this my last Will & Testamt. & I doe give & bequeath all that the Lord hath endowed me wth. in this world both Servts., catell, horses & hoggs & all my goods that is to me belonging & to faithfully pay them small debts that I owe & to give me decent buriall this being my last Will & Testamt. & doe disanull all former Wills by me formerly made I have hereunto sett my hand & seale this 9th day of Janu: in the year of or: Lord 1685
Testes THOMAS RANE   JAMES YEATS
       ROWLAND THORNTON,
       JOHN ◇ JACKSON
    Wee the Subscribers doe depose & say that we saw the within named Testatr. signe seale & deliver the within Will as his last Will & Testamt. & that he was of perfect sence & memory at the signing sealing & publishing of the same
                                                    THOMAS RANE
                                                    ROWLAND THORNTON
    Probatr p Sacrat: RAIN et THORNTON in Cur Com Rappa 3 die Martii 1685/6

pp.   AN INVENTORY of all & singular the Estate goods Debts Creditts & paps of Con-
90-   cerne late of Mr: JNO. SAMPSON deceased as they were exhibilled to us whose
95   names are hereunto Subscribed by Mr. WM. SLAUGHTER and apprized in pur-
       suance of an Ordr. of Rappah: Court on our oaths to the best of or: Judgments the
19th day of Jan: 1685/6 & are as followeth Vizt.

Imprimis. Bill taken in Capt: JNO. PURVIS name; EDWARD LEWIS, WM. BROCKNBROUGH
RICHD. JASPER, JNO. MASSEY, RICHD. KING, JNO. BATTIN, JNO. BAYLY, ISAAC WRIGHT,
RICHD. WITHITER pr Bill seale but not subscribed before Witness ANTHONY BILLINGTON;
PETER ELLIS, JAMES ORCHARD, JNO. PARTRIDGE & DAVID FRISTOE; EDWD. JEFFERY in
money

An Accot. of severall Debts entred in a Pockett Book in ye year 1683: JOHN BOWLES in
money, Ditto to Tobb: RICH: KING in money, MARTIN HAMMOND ditto to Tobb: JNO.
SMOOTT ditto to Tobb: ALEXLANDR. NEWMAN, DOMINICK RICE ditto in Tobb: JNO. BAYLEY,
DENNIS CARTY, JNO. ONELY, Coll. LEROY GRIFFIN, THO. BAYLIS; RICHD. PEACOCK, EDWIN
CONWAY, Mr. SAM: PEACHEY, ditto to Tobb: THO: GLASCOCK, JNO. TAVERNER, JAMES
SAMFORD, ISAAC more than his Bill above. 83 Mrs. TABITHA BOWLER (85) RODERICK
JONES, SAM; BAYLY, WM: STONE, JNO. SHERLOCK, ROB: TOMLIN JUNR., JAMES
ORCHARD, EDWARD JONES, A small Silver Seale; RICHD. WINTER, LUKE PLAY, RICH:
APPLEBY, ROBT: BAYLIS JUNR., JNO. SOAPER

An Accompt. of Debts in ye Day Book
RALPH WHITEING, WM. CROSSWELL, DANIELL HORNBY in both bookes; RICHD.
HUTCHINGS, WALTER PAVY one per of beds & furniture & 8 1/3 bushells of Salt; Coll.
WM. LOYD, JNO. MAISEY, RALPH DOWNING, PETTER ELLIS, ROBT. WALTER, THOMAS
BAYLIS, RICHD: PEACOCK, ROBERT DAVIS; JNO. TAVERNER

In the Longest Booke
GILES WEBB, THO: THOMPSON, DAN: HORNBY more, Mr. MALACHY PEALE, NATH. TURCKE
In the same booke are severall accts. of goods sold ffor Capt. JOHN PURVIS & Accompts.
HENRY NASH in mony and in Tobb: JOB HAMOND, DENNIS CARTY, HENRY LEWCAS,
DOCTR. ROGER WATER, JNO. OAKELY one barrall of Salt; Coll. LEROY GRIFFIN, THOMAS
BREAD, Majr. HENRY SMITH, RICHD. GLOVER, Mr. THO: TAYLOR, JNO. RICHARDS, JNO.
OVERTON, ISAAC WEBB, WALTER PAVY, ALEXR. ATTKINS, JAMES PERRY, Mr. CHARLES
DACRES, JNO. HERBERT, RICE EVANS, JNO. RICE, MICHAELL WILSON in a great book

Things Valiued in ready money. 2 Gold Rings; 2 pr old fashion embroydered Gloves, a
pen knife, a sun diall Brass ring; 2 bands for Wom: & 2 handkercheifs & a parcell of
band strings, a linnen bagg, Chest, butter pott; 2 pr of french falls; 1 sea rugg &
feather pillow, a cane & whipp, a pcell of books, a dale box & severll. small things in it;
a small looking glass, 2 razors, 4 old ffashion cravatt, a small trunck, a sweet powder
bagg, wearing linnen, 3 pillow beers & a towell, one black searge suit & pr of stockings,
other wearing appareli, a pcell of thred & some old stockings, a book the Authour
CLARKE, a pr of brass scales and one pound weight; a knife, an old saddle & old sifter,
old pr of Stillards not good, prcell of Joyners & Turners tooles, severall goods at Mr.
SUGGETTs taken from Mr. SAMPSONS STORE, one small silver sack cupp, a small Bible
with silver clasps, 2 small book Autr: JNO. & FRA: QUARLES, 1 pr of mens falls shoes & 1
pr of boys this Country make, head stall & reines of Virga. leather; one Nagg, 160 lb. of
sugar, an old Dutch case; 17 bushells of Salt, 23 Galls. of Rum, one pewter spirit pott, a
bedstead, one half bushell measure, 6 bushells of wheat

An Accot: of severall goods believed to be left with Mr. SAMPSON p Capt. JNO. PURVIS
Shoes, 5000 pins, gilt buttons, knives, thred lace, narrow tape, browne thread, whited
brown thred, small Ivory combs, Galloon, Kersey, Broad Cloth

In the Lesser Chest: 2 bed & bolster tickings, a horse whipp, a kerb bridle, thread, 1

doz. of Alcamy spoones, thred buttons, colored silk, hilling hoes, grubbing and weeding hoe, goose shott, 13 felt hatts No. D, 3 felt hatts No. 2; 3 felt hatts No. B; 2 felt hatts No. C., 2 other felt hatts, Ginger, hobb nailes, 6000 6d nailes, a great chest with lock & key; 92 books of the Country Law printed for J. PRICE have left unapparaized in the condition we found them in a Chest   Sum totall in money   20 lb. 09 01 1/2
Tobb: 36361 1/2

JNO. RICE
JNO. BAYLY
JNO. TAVERNER

Mr. WM. SLAUGHTER & the Apprizers subscribed & sworne the 19th day of January 1685 before me   SAM: PEACHEY
Recordtr. 16 die Martii 1685/6

p.   July 31st 1685.
95   AN INVENTORY of the Estate of JNO. ALEXANDER taken by us the Subscribers obedience to the within Ordr. of Court & apprized as followeth:
Impr. To horse colt; To coate & breeches; to 5 yds of Linsey Woolsy, To 1 pr of boots & fur single both old; To 5 yds more of Linnen Course; To 1 pr of shoes & hose
This Inventory taken the day & year as above p us
Sworne before me   PAUL WOODBRIDGE
9br the 23d 1685   WM. FITZHERBERT
        LEROY GRIFFIN
Recordt. 16 die Martii 1685

pp.   IN THE NAME OF GOD Amen. I FRANCES GODSON being sick & weake in body but
95-   in perfect memory do make this my last Will and Testamt. in manner & forme
96   as followeth:
    1. I bequeath my Soule to the hands of Almighty God my Creator & Maker in full and assured hopes of Salvation in & through the meritorious death & Passion of my deare & beloved Saviour Jesus Christ
    2. I bequeath my body to the Earth from whence it came to be Christian like buried by the discretion of ffriends
    3. I give & bequeath all my worldly goods Estate both reall & personall in manner & forme as followeth
    4. I give & bequeath all the mony that is due to me by Rappa County Court records to be equally divided between TOBY SMITH & HEN: SMYTH and their heires for ever
    5. I give & bequeath unto HEN: SMYTH all my Estate of land that is joyning to BRIDGETTs land, it being to the sd HENRY SMYTH & his heires forever
    6. I give & bequeath unto Mrs. ELIZABETH SMYTH all other things of my Estate and what may come out of England from my Unkle, to her own & proper use and behalf
    In Witness whereof I have sett my hand & fixed my seale this 27th day of January 1685/6
Signed Sealed & delivered in the prsence of
    GERARD ℰ FITZGERRALD.   FRANCES O GODSON
    EDW: ADCOCK
Wee the Subscribers do depose & say that wee saw the within Testatrx. signe & publish the above Will as her last Will & Testamt. & that at the signing & publishing the same she was of perfect sence & memory to the best of our knowledge and further saith not
                        EDWARD ADCOCK
                        GARRETT T FITZGERALD
Probatr p Sacrament Com in Cur Com Rappa 7 die Aprillis 1686

pp.   According to Order of Court bearing date the 3 day of March 1685/6 wch: saith
96-   that wee the Subscribers meeting at the House of Mr. WM. BANDRY shall sepa-
97   rate & sever the Estate of FRANCES MOSS from the Estate of her Sister, ELIZABETH
haveing in the sd Separacon due regard to the Inventory before made that the
sd FRANCES may as neer as possible have her part & portion of the sd Estate in kinde as
it was delivered have accordingly made separation sett out & divided the sd Estate as
followeth:

Imprs.To her part of Pewter, spoones, table linen, sheets, chaires, brass and potts in
the Kitching; Lumber in the Celler; her part of the Payles pans bedding particulars in
the milk house, to one Still to her part of Gun, one horse, her part of cattle, cowes, two
draught oxen, To Tobb: due for her part of a Womans Service; To one mantle, To her part
of Wool, sheep, Ewes, a wicker baskett, To Tobb: due to her from WM. BENDREY to make
up the sum   Errors Excepted   Sum Total 14194
                        HEN: AWBREY   GEO: TAYLER
                        SAMLL. BLOMFIELD JAMES HARRISON

Recordt. Cur Com Rappa 22 die April 1686

pp.   Rappa SS. By virtue of an order of Court to us ANTHO: NORTH, JNO. WELLS, THO:
97-   PARKER & RALPH ROWSEY directed bearing date the 3d of February 1685/6 wee
100   mett at the house of Mr. JOHN DANGERFIELD & there did apprise the Estate of
GEORGE BOYCE deced as followeth the 10th of Febry. 1685/6

Imprs: One black mare; one black jaded Gelding, small bay nagg; one browne bay, old
mare, one old over ridden Gelding, one parcell of old horse furniture bridles & sadle &c.
old dimety Drawrs: & old linen coats, one parcell of old neck Linen sleeves Ruffells, one
broad cloath crate breeches & Jackett, one serge coat & breeches, one Camlett Coat,
Ribbon, Carnation, Colored Orange, 3 knolts of penny damnified parcell gallome, old
sleeve slings, 1 remnant fillitting, Lace, shagg, silk strips, taffata, printed Callicoe,
Sivler Lace, black Taffatea; 6 ells holland, Callicoe course canvas, parcell shoes, 1 doe
skin, a parcel of shreds & twists of Tobb:, 3 pair new Stockings, 3 pare old stockings; 1
old trunk, Thread and old lumber theron, blue Linnen, Silk, parcell of thread, 4 caster
hatt & hat band; silk gimp, old buttons, stubbs of nayles, shreds of thred, one pare of old
scicers all in a Linen pockett, a Sword & belt, 3 pare old sheeres & 2 old parcell of Silver,
3 gold rings, an old Chest & peices of books lacerated; two pare gloves   9362

Bills due to the Testator: WM. HALSEY for 3 pare of Shooes; ROBT. READING, Mr.
SAMLL. BLOMFIELD, MARTIN JOHNSON JUNR., WM. BENDRY, ARTHUR ONEBY; JNO.
BATTAILE; WM. CARTER; GEO: MACKARLE, NATHLL. ALLEN, NICHO. PUTLEE; JNO. LIBB;
ROWLAND THORNTON, ANTHO: CARNABY, JNO. BROOKS, Capt. JOHN LAND, JNO. FERGUSON;
JNO. STEWARD, ARTHR. FORBES, WM. FITZHUGH Judgmt., on a new suit; JNO. GOODRICH
one days att: Subpena; Execr. vs. ED: DAVIS with: costs

Debts by Accot: Mr. WATSON, ROBT RUDDIFORD, (blank) BATES, ROBT. MILLS, MR.
TANDY JUNR., WM. HARDING, PHILL PENDLETON, WIDDOW HARPER, THOS. THRESHLEY,
JOHN STRONG, EDWARD ROWSEY, Mr. DANGERFIELD, RICHD. NIGHTENGALL, Mr. HENRY
TANDY, RICHD. TAYLER, JOHN GATEWOOD, JOHN BACKHAM, WM. LINDSEY, HEN: REEVES,
JNO. PAGETT; RICHD. GOOGE; JNO. ALMOND, WM. TARRANT, Captt. SAMLL. BLOMFIELD,
MARMADUKE LOYD, WM. BENDREY, JNO. JONES, JNO. QUESTENBERRY, Mr. FOULKS, WM.
CARTER, EDWARD JONES to Execr. in his hands delivered to THO: PACEY; JOSEPH GOOD-
RICH, Mr. TANDYes Bill   277734

Bills Desperate due in GLOCESTER COUNTY by Assignment as follows:
JNO. MINDLEN assigned by JOHN PEACOCK, JNO. GILBERT Ass. by SARAH PEACOCK, RALPH
GREEN by Accot: JNO. C. MALPASS Ass. of SARAH PEACOCK, GEO: FRANES Ass. p ditto;
RICHD. MARKES Ass. p SARAH PEACOCK

Wee the Appraisers within named Sworne according to order of Court have valued &
doe return this Inventory to be the best of our Judgment to what was to our view presented this day. In Testimonie whereof we have set our hands
Memorand: 30 lb. Tobb: was written by Mistake
the 10th February 1685   ANTHY. NORTH   JNO. WELLS
                         THOS: PARKER   RALPH ROWSEY

   The sd Appraisers were sworne before me
       HEN: AWBREY
   Recordatr Cur Com Rappa 22 die Aprilis 1686

p.   May Court 1686
100   IN THE NAME OF GOD Amen. I JOHN BOWEN being sick of body yett thanks be unto
         God of perfect memory do make & ordaine this my last Will & Testament in man-
ner & forme as followeth:
   First I commend my Soule into the hands of Almighty God my Maker hopeing to be
saved by the merits of Jesus Christ my Redeemer & my body to the Christian buriall &
for my Temporall goods I dispose of them in manner & form as followeth.
   Imprimis. I give & bequeath unto my Son, MATHEW BOWEN & JOHN BOWEN, two hundred & fifty acres of land where now I live on to be equally divided between them when
please God they shall live to the age of twenty one years
   2. I give & bequeath unto my other two Sons, STEPHEN & ALEXANDER BOWEN, my part
of a parcell of land lying in the forke bought by ALEXANDER DONIFAN & my self of
GEORGE JONES containing Five hundred acres to be equally divided between them when
they shall live to the age of twenty one years and my Will is that if either of my Sons
should please God to die that then my Daughter to have his part of lands, and if any else
of my Sons should die or all the remainder of my Sons die that then my Daughter,
MARTHA, & the Child that my Wife goeth with all to have the above remaining part of
land
   3ly. I bequeath unto my Son, MATHEW BOWEN, my horse Jack. I also bequeath to my
Daughter, MARTHA, a young mare now running in the woods a gray colour she & her
increase forever
   I bequeath also unto my loving Wife a gray horse, Hector
   I give also a mare & two horses unto STEPHEN, JOHN & ALEXANDER and the child my
Wife goeth wth: the increase of sd Mare forever I give & bequeath also unto my loving
Wife & JOHN, STEPHEN & ALEXANDER, MARTHA & the Child my Wife goeth with all my
female cattle to be equally divided between them and for the male Cattle I bequeath
unto my loving Wife. I bequeath also to my loving Wife all the hoggs & what household
goods I have. Also I do make & ordaine my loveing Wife Executx: & my Son, MATHEW,
Executr: with her to see this my Will performed. In Witness whereof I have sett my
hand & Seale this first day of April 1686
Testes MOSES HUBBERT   JOHN ⚬⚬ BOWEN
       ALEXR. DONIPHAN,   his marke
       FRAN:⤳ WILLIAMS
Wee the Subscribers do upon Oath declare that wee saw the within Testatr: signe seale
& publish the within written Will as his last Will & Testamt. & that then he was of good &
perfect memory to the best of our knowledge and further sayeth not
                          ALEXANDR: DONIPHAN
                          MOSES HUBBERT
                          FRAN: ⤳ WILLIAMS

Probatr p Sact. DONIPHAN, HUBBERT et WILLIAMS 5 die Maii 1686
Coram JNO: STONE, WM. LOYD & SAMLL. BLOMFIELD Justiciaries

pp.   Whereas I EDWARD GUNSTOCKER being now designed upon an Expedition with
100-   the English against my Cuntrymen, the INDIANS, do make ordaine constitute &
101   appoint this my last Will & Testament revokeing all other Wills either by word
         or writeing by me formerly made and this only to be accounted my last Will &
Testamt.
   Imprs. I do resigne my Soule to God & my body to the Earth. I doe make constitute &
appoint my beloved Wife, MARY GUNSTOCKER, my sole Executrx. and to her alone give &
bequeath my Plantacon & all housing thereunto belonging or appertaining my above
sd Plantacon containing One hundred & fifty acres wth. all my Stock of cattle & hoggs
younge & old with all my household goods and bedding & every moveable belonging &
appertayning to me. My above sd Wife paying all my due Debts. In Witness whereof I
have hereunto sett my hand & seale this Two & Twentieth day of October 1676
Signed Sealed & delivered in the presence of us
        JAMES KAY,   The marke of
        DAVID JONES,   EDWARD GUNSTOCKER   ⊓⊓⊓
        CHARLES HICKS   his Seale

p.   July Court 1686
101   IN THE NAME OF GOD Amen. I HENRY WILLOUGHBY Gent. do make this my last
         Will & Testament revokeing all former Wills by me made
   Imprs. I give my Soule to God & my body to the Earth
   Item I give & bequeath all my lands in Virginia to my Daughter, REBECCA HULL,
during her life & after her decease unto my two Grand Daughters, SARAH HULL &
MARY HULL, & their heires for ever
   Item The rest of my Estate I give unto my Daughter, REBECCA HULL, who I make
Executr: of this my last Will & Testamt. Witness my hand & Seale this 28th day of 9ber
1685
Sealed & delivered in presence of
        (none shown)   (No signature)
   Decembr: 21th: 1686. Mr. CHARLES HARRIS & EDWARD NESBUTT did in Court upon Oath
declare that Mr. HENRY WILLOUGHBY did in their hearing owne that this was his Will &
Testamt. & died before he could signe the same
   Vera Copia Teste THO: HOBSON JUNR. Cl Cur North
   Recordt Cur Com Rappa xxi die July 1686

pp.   Rappa SS. AN INVENTORY of all & singular the goods & Estate late of DOCR.
101-   HENRY WILLOUGHBY deced taken & appraised by us whose names are hereunto
102   subscribed by virtue of an order of Court dated the 3d day of March last & is as
         followeth Vizt.
   Imprs. 6 Books of Phsick in folio; 14 Phisick books in Quarto; 9 Phisick books in
Octavo, 16 Books of Phisick in XII, 6 History books in folio; 12 History books in Quarto,
most old, 15 other small books of avers subjects, a Bible in large Quarto; 2 books of
divinity in folio, 20 books of Divinity in Quarto; 27 books of Divinity in Octavo most old;
25 books of Divinity XVI; Books of the Law in folio; quarto in xvi; a parcell of lumber
in the Loft; an old Table, an old Court cubbard; & an old bedstead; 4 old trunks, 3 old
chests, an old desk & box, severall gaily potts & glass bottles & a box of small violls, 4
Iron wedges & 2 hand saws & two little hatchetts & small auger, a gouge, a looking glass,
a leather Jack to drink in & a brush; parcell of old pewter, an old Pewter Still, old paire
of stilliards, his wareing linen, his other wareing apparrell, pare of Stirrup leathers &
halter for a horse, an old fire shovell & dripingpan & butter pott & stand Copper LImbed

& worme; pare of Iron frying pan, Iron pott and an Iron pestle large & an Iron pestle & morter, pare of Tongues, a cross cut saw, old pare of bellows & an Iron ladle, an old feather bed, 2 feather pillows, a feather bolster & flock boulster, an old blankett & old coverled; an Ax & spade at Mr. PEACHEYs, small brass skillett at JNO. TAVERNERs, a young black stone horse now running & not at hand, a Bible at JOHN BATTINs, a Canvas bag in his house   6399

      JOHN SUGGETT   DAN: MA:CARTY
Sworne the last day of May 1686   JNO. BAYLEY
                                             SAMLL. TRAVERS
Bills: JOHN DERY , RODRICK JONES, PETER ELDER & RICHD. PEACOCK, THO: MASON, SAMLL. WALLOW; Mr: SAMLL. TRAVERS
Recordt. Cur Com Rappa xxii die July 1686

p.   Rappa SS. AN INVENTORY of the Estate of DANLL. MALLEY lately deced taken
103   by WM. PAYNE the 3d day of July 1686
       Imprs. 6 yds kersey, 3 pare mens french falls, 1 felt hatt; serge, 1 serge coat halfe worn, pare demity trowsers, 2 pares dowlas trowsers, a dimity wastcoat 2 striped handkerchus, 1 peice white filitting, browne thread, red ribbon, black ditto, 1 Ivory Comb, whited brown thread, 24 skeynes of Silk, 1/2 gross of Silk & gimp buttons, 1 pare corduvant gloves, 9 yds. of dyed linen, 2 shillings Sterling, 1 Chest, 1 hilling hoe; dowlas, white dimity, canvas, 9 yds. Scotch cloth, 15 yds blu Lenen; 2 dowlas Shirts, 2 pare new worsted Stockings, 1 pare old ditto, 1 weeding hoe; 1 narrow ax, 3 bills each cont: 450 lb Tobb: 1f lock bed bolster, rug & coverlett, 2 cowes, 1 heyfer 2 years old, 1 steer 1 yeare old, 2 cow yearlings, 2 mares, 1 yearling Coult, 1 Sadle & bridle, 1 pare spurs & whip, 1 pare white yarne stockings
The Subscriber being indebted to the Estate 70 lb. of Tobb: & a barrell of Corne
          Taken by me   WILLIAM PAYNE
Recordt. Cur Com Rappa xxii die Julii 1686

pp.   August Court 1686
103-   AN INVENTORY taken this 5th day of June 1685 of the Estate of JOHN BUTLER
104   deced.
       Imprs. A parcell of old Caske & gally potts, 2 old iron potts, a grid iron and pare of iron tongues & some old iron; an old warming pann, a looking glass & a brass candlestick, a small parcell of pewter, a Table & a forme & 3 old Chayres, an old flock bed & blankett & coverled and old chest & bedstead, one gun & a pistoll, a mare & foale, a parcell of books, 2 pewter dishes, an Iron dripping pan, a Cabinett, a box iron & small trunk; a brass kettle, a flock bed & boulster & blanketts, a sadle & halsters, a chest, a heyfer of 3 yeares old, 1 heyfer of 2 yeares old & cask
  In obedience to an order of the Worshpll. Court of the County of Rappa. We have appraised the Estate of JOHN BUTLER   CHARLES JOHNSON
                                         ROBT: PLEY
                                         JA: BOULEWARE

Recordt. Cur Com Rappa 13 die Augusti 1686

p.   August Court 1686
104   IN THE NAME OF GOD Amen. I MAGDALEN GIBSON of the County of Rappa being
       sick & weake of body but of perfect sence & memory doe make this my last Will & Testamt.
     Imprs. I bequeath my Soule to God that gave it & my body to the dust from whence it

was taken in hopes of Resurrection to Life at the last day through our Lord & Saviour Jesus Christ & dispose of my temporall estate in manner & forme following

It. I give & bequeath unto my Son, TOBIAS INGRAM, & to his first Child lawfully begotten of his own body, all & singular my whole Estate to be equally hand & enjoyed between them saveing such legacys Exceptions & Cautions hereunderneath sett down alwaise provided in case of the death of the sd Child that then the second Child of my son or the Third Child wch: shall be the Eldest Survivour shall enjoy my Estate joyntly with my Son as abovesd but what Stock of hoggs I have I will that my Son, TOBIAS INGRAM, hve hold and enjoy them to his own proper use & behoof saveing Six sowes & foure barrows wch I will that he pay unto his sd Child in Copartnership with him at the time that it shall attaine the age of Eighteen years

Item I give & bequeath unto JOHN GRAY one horse (Vizt) a gray gelding branded about 3 years old

Item I give & bequeath unto ARABELLA WHITE one heyfer of a yeare old

Item I will & ordaine & appoint my Son, TOBIAS INGRAM, to be Executr: of this my last Will & Testamt., joyning with him, JOHN GRAY, as Overseer & Assistant

Item I do revoke annull & make void all former Will or Wills by me had or made & do appoint this & none other to be my last Will and Testamt: & in Testimony hereof I have hereunto signe with my hand & affix my seale & Publish this my last Will & Testamt. in presence of lawfull witnesses this 7th day of Septembr: 1685
Signed Sealed and Published
     THO: PARKER,   (no signature)
     NATHLL. ALLEN

Wee whose names are here underneath subscribed do depose & say that in our sight & hearing the within mentoned Testatrx: did signe seale & publish this within Will & declare it to be her last Will & Testamt.   NATHLL. ALLEN
                                                THO: PARKER

Probatr. in Cur Com Rappa 4 die Augusti 1686 et Recordt. 13 die

pp.   Rappa. County. AN INVENTORY & Appraisemt. of the Estate of JOHN COLLINS, late
104-   of the sd County deced taken & appraised in pursuance of an Order of the sd
106   County Court dated the 7th July 1686 to us THO: HARWAR, WM. YOUNGE, DANLL.
       DOBBINS directed as the sd Estate was to us presented to veiw by ROBERT WEBB
being thereunto sworne by Order of the sd Court the 10th July 1686 as followeth, Viz.

Imprs. Two Negro men, one man Servant about a yeare & half, one Boy about 3 yeares, one woman Servant about 1 year 8 months, one horse, 18 high leathered Chaires, 2 low wooden chaires, parcell of pewter dishes, plates & basons weighing eighty five pounds, Iron pottangers, three Chamber potts, a parcell of hollow pewter, two brass candlesticks, two brass skilletts, one old Lanthorne, 2 old tin pepper boxes, twelve old wooden Trenchers, three earthen muggs, one old tin sauce pan & funnell, one fire shovell & tongues, twenty six glass bottles, one small gun; one pare stilliards prized & can hooks, five old tin pans, 3 earthen butter potts about a pound & half of cotten weike & an old case of bottles, a table & looking glass, feather bed and furniture & bed stead, an old flock bed blankett, Match coat and Canvas ticking, tin pailes, parcell of old linen, seventeen Napkins & towells & three table cloths, two pare canvas sheets, one pare fine ditto, two pare pillow bers, one small brass kettle, eleven pare of small wool cards, one old poare of stilliards & prize, one ax and two hammers, 3nd 10: nayles, 3nd 6do, 3d: 20 do; 6 lb 8 do, 6 lb 4 do, one iron pott & pott hooks, one pott rack, one hook, one iron pestle, one flesh fork, one grid iron, one spitt & one fry pan, one broad ax, one old spade, 1 old falling ax, some iron vedges, one hand saw, one iron candle stick, 23 yards narrow blue, eleven yards course kersey, foure pare Childrens bodies, 12 pare Childrens stockings, 6 yds serge, 5 yards canvis course colored cotten, 7 nd 1/2 pinns, one parcell of knives, a parcell of colored thredd & a little blue tape, 4 horne combes, 3 pare sissers, a parcell of hob nayles, two pare of boys plain shooes & one pare of childs shooes, sixteen yards course kersey, foure deer skins, 32 ells linen, three old small chests, one box smoothing iron & heaters, one barrill course panncell sugar, one parcll. Ditto, one grind stone, one callico carpet   Sum totall   19756

The aforemenconed appraismt. amounts to Nineteen thousand seven hundred and fifty six pounds of Tobb: was by us the appraisers taken & valued the day within written Witness our hands   THO: HARWAR
                                                       WM. YOUNGE
                                                       DANLL. DOBYNS

The aforemenconed appraisers and the sd ROBT. WEBB sworne the 15th July 1686 before me   HENRY WILLIAMSON
Recordt. Cur Com Rappa xxi die Augusti 1686

p.   THE INVENTORY & Appraisemt. of the Estate of BARNABY WELLS deced p Order
106   of the Worshipll. Court by us whose names are here subscribed July the 21st
         1686
One old horse, old couch, old fry pan, small flock bed boulster blanketts & old rugg: old sheet, parcell of old Coopers tooles, old gun, old bed & two old ruggs, one small tray & two old trayes very old, two old potts & one small kettle, one quartr. Caske & one small Rundlett   985
Sworne before mee the day & yeare
above written   the marke of
      GEO: TAYLER   GRACE ⬭ WELLS
                                      the marke of   Λ   JOHN FENNELL
                                      the marke of   O   THO: NEWMAN

Recordt. Cur Com Rappa xvii die 7bris 1686

pp.   AN ACCOMPT of that part of Cattle & Pewter belonging to FRANCES, one of the
106-   Orphans of Mr. WM. MOSS deced as it was divided by us the Subscribers this
107   12th day of February 1685/6
         Vizt. 3 heyfers of 2 yeares old each; 3 steeres 5 years old each, the one red the other blackish browne with a star in the forehead and white belley; 2 heyfers 3 years old the tayles cutt; 1 bull 3 yeares old, 1 steere 3 years old, 2 yearling, 5 cows & one calfe the cowes are named as followeth: Fidler, Star, Fanin, Ratt & Tidey; Also there is on quartr: of a Bull of 6 years old & the half of a yearling belonging to her share; and a steere of 6 years old wch: was killed by Mr. WM. BROWNE who marryed the sd FRANCES MOSS

An Account of the Pewter also belonging to the sd FRANCES is as followeth: 6 new plates & foure old dishes, 7 new Potangers, 2 old Potangers, 1 new Flaggon, 1 new Salt, 1 new Chamber pott, 1 great old bason, 1 old dish, 4 new broad dishes, Conr. 33 pounds
Divided by us the subscribers according to Order of Court bearing date the last Novembr: 1685
Sworne to before me the date abovesd   ALEXANR: DONIPHAN
      GEORGE TAYLER   CHAS. X WILSON
                                                       CHPL. ASLCOUGH
                                                       THO: NEW

Recordr. Cur Com Rappa xvii die 7bris 1686

pp.   Rappa. ss. Octo. Court 1686
107-   AN INVENTORY & Appraisement of the Estate of WILLIAM FANTLEROY deced
109   taken & appraised by virtue of an Order of the sd County Court as the same was
         presented to us the Appraisers by KATHERINE, the Widdow Relict & Admx. of the
said WM. the 4th day of Septembr: 1686

ATT THE ISLAND QUARTER: Five cowes & calves, 4 yearlings, one heifer four years old,
two iron potts & pott hooks, one iron pestle, one old frying pan, one old hand saw, three
old hoes & iron brand, one Servant named WM. GREENHILL about twenty two months to
serve; 130 foot of Inch & half plank; 225 foot of Inch board, an old tenant saw, an old
whip saw & an ax

ATT THE DWELLING HOUSE in Mr. FANTLEROYs CHAMBER:
Two tables & one old Chest, 16 yds Scotch cloth, 4 yds. blue Callicoe, 3 ells course cotten;
one cotten coverled, one suit Callico curtaines & valence; all the deceds wearing apparrell, linen, woolen hatt, stockings & shooes, a parcell of thred laces, silk wast coat, &
small trifles, a parcell of trifles in the Cubbard, an old desk & two glass cases, pare of old
bellows, an old box Iron & heater

IN THE HALL CHAMBER a little table wth a Drawer & a warming pan

IN THE PORCH CHAMBER One flock bed, rug, boulster, blanketts, bed stead, curtaines &
vallance, two rush chaires & one old chest

IN THE CHAMBER OVER Mr: FANTLEROYs CHAMBER: Two small block beds, one old bedstead, two old ruggs & blanketts, two old saddles

IN THE CELLER. A parcell of earthen ware, six doz: of empty bottles, Ninety gall. of
Rum; 25 gals. Lime Juice, twelve doz: bottles of wine; one barrell of Tarr

IN THE HALL CLOSETT. An old iron & small pare of old stilliards, 12 sickles, a parcell of
old earthen potts and old box & a pare small old skates; one Negro woman named Bess,
one very old Negro man & very old Negro woman, one man Servant named JAMES
FOUNTAIN about a yeare to serve & to have four hundred pounds of Tobb: Extraordinary.
One woman Servt. about 3 years to serve, a very old leaky Boat old rotten sayles & oars, a
parcell of books, an old knife, a very old sunken sloop & old rotten riggin; 122 foot of
two Inch plank, 169 foot Inch plank, Twenty three Sheep at Colnll. SAMLL. GRIFFINs at
CHERRY POINT

IN THE KITCHIN. A Table & forme, a cheese press & small brass kettle, twelve old plates
& a pewter bason

It. JOHN SETTLEs Bill; WM: BARGIMANs Bill; ALEXANDR: NEWMANs Bill for one
hundred & twenty bushlls: of wheat

The totall of this Inventory amounts unto Thirty thousand eight hundred Twenty &
Eight pounds of Tobb: & one hundred & twelve bushlls: of Wheat

Wee GEO: TAYLER, SAMLL: PEACHEY, SAMLL: TRAVERS and SAMLL. BAYLEY the per-
sons appointed to take the before Inventory & appraise the sd Estate by Order of Rappa
County Court In Testimony of the truth of the same have subscribed our names the 4th
Septr: 1686   GEO: TAYLER
                                                     SAMLL: PEACHEY
                                                     SAMLL. TRAVERS
The aforemenconed Appraisers & the   SAMLL. BAYLEY
Admstrx. sworne the day & year aforesd
before me   WILL TAYLOE

Wee the Subscribers being appointed by Order of the Worspll. Court of Rappa County to
meet at ye house of Mr. WM. FANTLEROY deced to separate from the Estate all & singular
such Negroes, goods & household stuff as apperteyned to & menconed in a Schedule
annexed to a Certain Deed of Joynture made from the sd WM: to RICHD. LEE Esqr. &
LEROY GRIFFIN Gent. for the uses in the sd Deed menconed and to make report of what is

wanting or not in being the same to the said Court. Wee do finde that KATHERINE, the
now Widdow & Admistrx. of the sd WILLIAM by her own confession & acknowledgmt.
hath all the particulars menconed in the said schedule save only two mares two paire of
sheets & eighteen Napkins wch: wee accordingly report

Witness our hands the 4th of Sept. 1686

GEO: TAYLER
SAMLL. PEACHEY
SAMLL. TRAVERS
SAMLL. BAYLEY

Recordt. Cur Com Rappa xviii die 8bris 1686

p. IN THE NAME OF GOD Amen. I JOHN PALMER being sick in body but in perfect
109 minde and memory doe make this my last Will & Test: as followeth

Imprs. I bequeath my Soule to God who gave it hopeing in my Saviour Jesus
Christ for eternall salvation & my body to the Earth from whence it was taken with
convenient Christian buriall

Item I do make & appoint WM. BARBER to be my sole Executr: and doe order what I
have after debts paid & funerall charges that be taken care to send it to my Wife in
England only my wearing cloths I give to JOHN PETERSON In Witness whereof I hereunto sett my hand and Seale this 16th: of Septembr: 1686
Signed sealed in the presence of us

RALPH GRAYDON,   JOHN PALMER
JOHN S WELCH
JOHN S PETERSON

Wee the Subscribers do depose & say that we saw the within Testator signe seale &
publish the within Will as his last Will & Testament & that he was of perfect sence &
memory at the time of signing & sealing the same to the best of our knowledge &
further say not   JOHN PETERSON
                                             RALPH GRAYDON

Probatr p Sacramt. PETERSON et GRAYDON in Cur Com Rappa 6 die 8bris 1686

pp. TO ALL CHRISTIAN PEOPLE to whom these presents may or shall concern Know
109- yee that I JONAS PAGE being sick & weake of body but of perfect memory do
110 make this my last Will & Testamt.

Imprs. my Soule I bequeath unto God that gave it me & Jesus Christ my Redeemer my body I desire to be Christianly buried & for what I have I do give & bequeath
as followeth

It: I do make HENRY CLARK liveing in TOTASKEY CREEK my whole Executr: to take
into his hands all that portaing & belongs to me for such use as followeth. My two
mares & two colts I do give unto HENRY CLARKs Son unto the above HENRY CLARKE with
all the encrease hereafter; Likewise I do give unto sd HENRY CLARK younger seven
breeding Cattle & two male cattle the same being desired to remaine in the hands of his
Father, HENRY CLARKE, untill his Son is capable to make use of them himselfe. All this
I desire may be performed. In Witness whereof I have sett unto my hand & seale this
22d day of July Ano. 1686
Signed & sealed in prsence of us

RICHD. DUDLEY,   JONAS ⊤ P PAGE
THO: ⊙ DUDLEY,
HENRY ++ TILLEY

Wee the Subscribers do depose & say that wee saw the within Testatr: signe seale &
publish the within written Will as his last Will & Testamt: & that he was of perfect sence

& memory at the time of signing & sealing the same to the best of our knowledge &
further say not   RICHD: DUDLEY
                                                                  THO: ◯ DUDLEY

Probatr p Sacra: RICHARD DUDLEY et THOME DUDLEY in Cur Com 6 die 8bris 1686

p.   Apr: 1686. A Schedule or Inventory of the Estate of Mr: JOHN PALMER,
110   Comandr: of the KETCH, *LOVES INCREASE* of Virginia deced brought before us
         SAMLL: BAYLEY & RALPH GAYDEN, Appraisers appointed by an order of Court
bearing date the 6th day of this Inst. Octobr: and appraised by us this 20th day of
October 1686
   One peice of course serge; 11 yards of course ditto; a parcell of old books, one old chest
& one old QUADRANT, one old Sea Bed rugg & blankett, one pare of small stilliards 570
                                                                  SAMLL: BAYLEY
                                                                  RALPH GRAYDEN

Recordt. Cur Com Rappa 12 day die 9bris 1686

p.   IN THE NAME OF GOD Amen. First I bequeath my soule to God that gave it & my
110   body to decent buriall. I give unto my Daughter, SUSANNA, all my land and one
         red pied heyfer known by the name of Primrose
Secondly, I give unto WILLIAM WITT the first mare foale that my mare brings and all
the rest of my moveable Estate I give unto my loveing Wife as Witness my hand & Seale
this 11th day of January 1686/6
Test   JNO. HANSFORD,   THO: FULLER
       ZACHA ✝ HEFFORD
JOHN HANSFORD & ZACHARIA HEFFORD do make Oath the within named Testator was of
perfect sence & memory when he signed the within Will to the best of our knowledge
Witness our hands this 3 day of 9ber 1686
                                                                  JNO. KAWFORD
                                                                  ZACHARIA ✝ EFFORD

Probatr p Sacram 3d die 9bris in Cur Com Rappa

p.   IN THE NAME OF GOD Amen I ANN RICE, Widdow & Relict of DOMINICK RICE deced
111   being at this present sick in body but of perfect mind and memory doe make
         this my last Will and Testament following
Imprs. I bequeath my Soule to God who gave it hopeing in Jesus Christ my Saviour &
Redeemer for Eternall Salvation & my body to the Earth from whence it was taken with
convenient Christian buriall
   It. I do make & appoint my Son, THO: DUE to be my sole Executr: & do leave all my Chil-
dren to him during their minority desireing him only to be carefull of them, but in
case of mortallity of my Son, THO: DEW, the Children to be kept as aforesd by my Son,
ANDREW DEW, & if he should happen to die before the Children come to age that then
my Son, WM. TOONE, to take them in to his Custody untill they come to age
   It. I give unto my Daughter, ANN TOONE, all my wearing cloths
   It. I will & appoint my sd Executr: to act & doe in all things belonging to me in my
Husband DOM: RICEs last Will & Testamt: & to secure the Childrens Estate wch was for-
merly given unto them. In Testimony whereof I have hereunto sett my hand & seale
this 8th day of February 1684/5
Signed sealed & delivered in the presence of
       WM. BARBER,   A. R.
       JOSEPH JEFFERSON,
       SAMLL: WHITHEAD

I the Subscriber did see Mrs. ANN RICE signe seale & publish this as her last Will and Testaml: WM. BARBER
    Probatr p sacram BARBER in Cur Com Rappa 3 die 9bris 1686

pp.   AN INVENTORY taken of the Estate of HUMPHREY WHEELER deced August the
111-   15th 1686
112   Imprs. To foure sowes & ten shoats; four pr: old shooes, two pare yarne
           stockings; 2 knives & pare of gloves; 1 pare Drawers, 4 old shirts & a canvas
bagg, 2 old coats & old wastcoat; 3 neck cloths & parcell of thread; 2 old pewter dishes, a
Tankard & old Potangrs., one old Bible, two tin potts & looking glass; 1 smothing Iron &
cutting knive; one old hatt; 2 old boxes & a parcell of ginger; one old flock bed, 2 old
ruggs & old hamack; 1 silver Thimble, a silver Corrall; & old sifter, 10 bushlls. of
Indian Corne, 1 old chest & one old kettle, To Tobacco due to the Estate   1883
                 Errors Excepted
Inventory & appraised by us the day & year above written
                                         ARTHUR HODGES
                                         WM. FITZJEFFRIES
    The persons wch: have hereunto subscribed have sworne before me that the particu-
lars above menconed are by them appraised to the full value thereof to the best of their
Judgmts: this 27th day of 9bris 1686
                                         THO: EDMONDSON

    Recordt. 10 die 10bris 1686

p.   January Court 1686/7
112   IN THE NAME OF GOD Amen. I NATHANLL. GUBB being sick in body but of good
           & perfect memory blessed be God do appoint this to be my last Will & Testamt.
in manner & forme following
    Imprs. I give unto my Sister, MICHAH, all what came in the *EXETER MERCHANT,* this
yeare & all what is of Mr: THORNBURYs And to Mr. SWAN for his Mare fifteen hundred
pounds of Tobb: & to Colnll. LOYD fifty shillings which he lent me of wch some part is in
my Chest & I allow for my funerall charges Two thousand pounds of Tobo: And all Debts
being paid I do make my Mother whole & sole Executrix. of this my last Will & Testamt.
and after her decease all to my Cozens equally divided and this to be delivered to Mr.
JOSEPH HARINGER & Mr. ROBINSON, Attorney at Law, and for the due discharge of this I
do allow to them foure hundred & fifty pounds of Tobo: In Witness whereof I have
hereunto sett my hand & seale this 20th day of Novembr: 1686
Sealed & delivered in the presence of us
    JAMES SANFORD,   NATH: GUBB
    HEN: TAYLER
    I the Subscriber do upon Oath declare that I saw the within Testator signe seale &
publish the within Will as his last Will & Testamt: and that he was of sound & perfect
memory at the time of signing & sealing the same according to the best of my knowledge   JAMES SANDFORD
    Jurati est JAS SAMFORD in Cur Com Rappa 5 die Jan 1686/7

pp.   Virginia xber the 28th 1686
112-   IN THE NAME OF GOD Ame. I JOHN LINCOLN of Rappa County of Farnham Parish
113   being very sick & weeke of body but of perfect memory thanks be to God for it
           doth make this my last Will & Testamt: revoking all other Wills Testamts. in form
following

Imprs. I bequeath my Soule to Christ my Redeemer & my body to Christian buriall according to the discretion of my Executr. hereafter menconed

I doe give to my dear Wife, ELIZABETH, all what land I now am possessed of during her naturall life not to be destroyed by her & likewise a Childs part of all stock & moveables

I do give all my land unto my Son, JOHN, after his Mothers decease to be quietly possessed by him & likewise one young horse named Nabb branded with J: L: on the further buttock and two Cowes & calves marked with two crops & two slitts of the neare Eare one slitt of the right Eare & under keeled on the same with their encrease not to be removed of my now dwelling plantacon

I do give to my Daughter, ELIZ:, 1 mare big wth foale named Betty wth: her encrease, not to be removed as aforemenconed & two Cowes & calves marked as afore menconed wth their encrease not to be removed of my now dwelling plantacon

I do give to my Daughter, MARGARET, one younge horse named Ball of two years old and two cows and calves of the former marke with the encrease to remaine upon the now dwelling plantacon

I do give to my Daughter, CATHERINE, one mare called Pigg with her encrease with two cowes & calves with encrease not to be removed of my now dwelling plantacon

I do give to my four Children afore menconed and to each of them one Sow & two Barrows of one yeare age

(no signature)

Us the Subscribers are able to attest that this was the reall dictate of JOHN LINCOLN sensible to the last Word writeing and likewise that he did urge to have CHARLES DODSON to be his Executr: severall times when his Wife was named

JOHN M MILLS,   HENRY ++ HARTLEY
GILB: ⌂ CROSWELL WM: BRASEY

HENRY HARTLEY, JOHN MILLS & GILBERT CROSWELL made Oath to all & every the abovesd Will & Attestation by them signed the hoggs only excepted

Teste WM. COLSTON Cl.

Probatr in Cur Com Rappa 5 die Januarii 1686/7

p. 113   AN INVENTORY of the Estate of ROBT. CASH taken & appraised by us under written July the 26th 1686

Imprs. One small gunn, one broken carbine, one small Bible; 3 yards of wearing stuff; 1 pare of old stockings & one old felt hatt; a parcil of wearing stuff, 3 shirts, 1 handkercher, 1 pare plaine shooes, two yds Serge; 3 pare old breeches, 1 suit serge cloth; 1 case small pistoll, 1 small flock bed bolster rugg, 1 chest, 1 old trunk, parcell Carpenters tooles, another parcell of old tooles; 1 old gray horse not yett knowne whither it be CASHes, one bay horse & armes

Sworne before me this 1st January 1686   FRAN: SLOUGHTER
        SAMLL: BLOMFIELD   MARTIN JOHNSON

Recordatr. Cur Com Rappa 19 die Januarii 1686/7

pp. 113- 114   IN THE NAME OF GOD Amen. I JOHN WITHERS of Rappa County being sick & weake in body but of perfect sence & memory of minde praised be God therefore, do make this my last Will & Testamt: in manner & forme following.

I give & bequeath my Soule into the hands of Almighty God my Creator hopeing to be saved by the Merritts of my Saviour Jesus Christ my body I order to be buried with Christian buriall by my Executrx. hereafter named as for my worldly goods I give & bequeath them in manner & forme following

Imprs. I do will & desire that whatsoever of goods or Estate I am seized of after my de-

cease as soone as can be conveniently be equally divided into three parts whereof my
Will is the one part so divided be reserved & kept for my Daughter, MARGARETT
WITHERS, to be possessed by her when she shall come to ye age of Sixteen years else the
day of Marriage wch shall first happen; the other two parts I give into my well beloved Wife, SARAH WITHERS, for the use as well of her selfe as also for the Child with
which she now goeth & is with Child of whether it be male or female to be equally
divided also my desire & will is that my Wife shall have the keeping of my Daughter,
MARGARETT WITHERS, in her own Custody whom I ordaine the sole Executrx. of this my
last Will and Testamt: as well in paying as receiving & in all other cases. In Witness
whereof I have hereunto sett my hand & seale this second day of Aprill in the year of
our Lord 1686
Being prsent at the signing & sealing
& delivery of these presents   JOHN ⨎ M WITHERS
        THO: KENDALL;
        JOHN ⊗ CROW,
        WM. HEATHER
   January the 5th 1686. I WM. HEATHER attest upon Oath that I saw the within named
Will signed sealed & delivered by the within JOHN WITHERS as Witness my hand
                                                        WM. HEATHER

   I JOHN CROW do attest upon Oath that I saw the within menconed Will signed sealed &
delivered by the within named JOHN WITHERS as Witness my hand the day & year above
written   JOHN ⊗ CROW his marke
   Probatr pr HEATHER & CROW in Cur Com Rappa 5 die January 1686/7

pp.   March Court 1686/7
114   THE LAST WILL of LUKE BILLINGTON deced the 25th of January 1686 first be-
115   queathing his Soule to God Almighty and his body to the ground &c.
         It. I bequeath to TEIGE McDONNOGH my sword & belt with all my wearing cloths
   It I bequeath to my Cousens the remainder of my Estate (after my Sister, BARBARA &
SAMLL. BAYLY are paid) equally to be divided between them
   It. my Brass Pistolls to Little DANNIELL.
   It. my Turkey Barrell Gun to WM. ROBINSON but after a little better Collection of his
sences bequeathed the same to his Brother, CARTY, saying that he thought he would
have nothing else
   It. To AN ROBINSON I would leave some thing but what I can not tell but upon some
small recollection bequeathed her the first mare foale that any of his Mares brought
                                        TEIGE MACKDONNOGH
                                        LAWRENC HUMMINGS
   March 2d 1686/7 Sworne in Rappa County Court by MACKDONNOGH & HUMMINGS
                    Test WM. COLTON Cl Cur
But after two or three hours were past & his Brother, CARTY, was gott out of his bed &
asked him how he did he replyed he was in differenh well. Mr: CARTY said Brothr: I
understand you made a Will & he replied yes, then Mr. CARTY demanded whether he
remember his Will and desired that he may hear him repeat it, he replyed it so began as
followeth. I give my Cloths sword & belt to the Irishman and the first mare foale that
any of my Mares bring to ANN ROBINSON and after my Debts are paid the residue of my
Estate to be equally divided between my five Cozens. The Mr. CARTY demanded what five
cozens and he replyed I meane my foure Couzens which be them sd Mr. CARTY. He
made answer yor: three Children & ROBT. BAYLYEs Child. And I think I ow SAMLL.
BAYLY Two thousand weight of Tobb: or thereabouts. Then Mr. CARTY demanded whom

do you appoint to performe yor: will & he replyed whom should I but you for I think
you have most right to it. And after yor: death, SAMLL. BAYLY if he survives you is to
see it performed & over see it till the Children comes of age and my Horse Turke I leave
him also Then Mr. CARTY demanded do you leave him the horse over & above his Debt &
he replyed yes

LAWRENCE ⓢ HUMMINGS

March 2d 1686/7 Sworne in Rappa County Court by LAW. HUMMINGS
Probatr. in Cur Com Rappa 2 die Martii 1686/7 el Recordalr

p.   January 22, 1686
115   IN THE NAME OF GOD Amen. I THOMAS TAYLER being sick & weake of body but
       of perfect memory do here make my last Will & Testamt. Imprs. I bequeath my
soule to Almighty God that gave it and my body to have such decent buriall in the Earth
as my Executrs. shall think fitt.

It. I give to each of my Godsons, JOHN PAVINER JUNR. & SAMFORD JONES one thousand
pounds of tobb:

It. I give to ISAAC WEBB, Sone of JOHN WEBB, one thousand pounds of Tobb:

It. I give to friend REES EVANS one thousand pounds of Tobb:

It. I give to THOMAS WHITE foure hundred pounds of Tobb:

It. I give to ELIZ. POND foure hundred pounds of Tobb:

It. I cleerly discharge & sett free my Boy Servant, THO: HEWETT, giveing him my
wollen & Linin cloths

It. I give Six pounds Sterling to my friends Mr. ED: JONES, Mrs. ELIZ. JONES, Mr. THO:
BAYLIS, Mrs. CATHERINE BAYLIS, Mr. JOHN WEBB & Mr. ISAAC WEBB each of them
Twenty Shillings of the above sd money and desire each of them to buy a Ring of the
value

I will & order Mr. JAMES SAMFORD & Mr. WM. COLSTON to be Executrs: to this my last
Will & Testamt.

Signed & Sealed in the prsence of us
     ISAAC WEBB,   THO: TAYLER
     JOHN BLAKE,
     JOS: ✕ DAVIS

Wee the Subscribers do make Oath that the within Testatr. did signe seale & publish the
within Will as his last Will & Testamt: & that he was of perfect sence & memory at the
signing & sealing of the same & further say not   ISAAC WEBB
                                         JOHN BLAKE

Probatr. Sacra: WEBB & BLAKE in Cur Com Rappa 2 die Martii 1686/7

pp.   IN THE NAME OF GOD Amen. I WILLIAM TRAVERS of Rappa. County Gent. being
115-   weake & sick of body but of perfect sence Judgmt: & memory Almighty God be
116   praised do make & appoint this my last Will & Testamt: revokeing all other for-
       mer Wills whatsoever in manner & forme following Vizt.

Imprs. I bequeath my Soule to Almighty God that gave it trusting that through the
merits of his Son and my deare Saviour Jesus Christ he will be pleased gratiously to
receive it into his Kingdom there to live with him evermore and I committ my body to
the ground to be decently buried

It. I give & bequeath unto my dear Mother, REBECCA RICE, five thousand pounds of
Tobb: dureing her naturall life to be left in the hands of my Brother, SAMUEL TRAVERS,
to be at her disposall when she shall be pleased to call for it & after her death to return
to my sd Brothr: SAMLL. TRAVERS, & RAWLEIGH TRAVERS their heires Executrs.

Adminstrs. &c.

It. I bequeath unto my Father in Law, JOHN RICE, my riding horse wth furniture

It. I give to KATHERINE REYLEY Five hundred pounds of Tobb: in Caske

It. I give & bequeath unto SAMLL. ROBINSON, Son of ELIAS ROBINSON, one heifer wch: is at the house of JOHN BALLIN with all her increase & if the sd SAMLL. shall die before he arrives to the age of one and twenty years that then it shall returne to the said ELIAS ROBINSON the Father of the sd SAMLL.

It. I give & bequeath all the rest of my Estate unto my two loveing Brothers, SAMLL: & RAWLEIGH TRAVERS, their heires Executrs. Admistrs: forever equally to be divided between them. My Will is that if my Father in Law, Mr. JOHN RICE, pay fifteen thousand pounds of Tobb: as part of my Estate unto my sd Loveing Brothers their heirs or order on the 10th day of March which will be in the year of our Lord 1687/8 that then he shall have the Liberty to pay the remayning part from thence untill the tenth day of October wch: will be in the yeare of our Lord God 1689.

It. I do constitute & appoint my two loveing Brothers, SAMLL. & RAWLEIGH TRAVERS, my lawfull Executrs. of this my last Will and Testament. In Witness whereof I have hereunto sett my hand & fixed my Seale the 14 day of Febry. 1686/7

Signed Sealed & delivered in the presence of

WM: SLOUGHTER,   WM. TRAVERS
GEO:-+- BAKER
JOANNA GRAYDEON

I the Subscriber doe make oath that I saw the above & within Testator signe seale & publish the within & above Will as his last Will & Testamt: & that he was of perfect sence & memory at the time of signing & sealing the same & further saith not

GEO: -+- BAKER
WM. SLOUGHTER

As above so deposeth
Probatr in Cur Com Rappa 2 die Martii 1686/7

pp. 116-117   IN THE NAME OF GOD Amen. I RICHARD CAUTHURNE of the Parish of Sittenburne in the County of Rappa in Virginia Plantr. being in health praised be given unto God for the same & knowing the uncertaintie of this Life on Earth and being desirous to settle things in order do make this my last Will & Testament in manner & forme following:

That is to say, principally I commend my Soule unto Almighty God my Creator assuredly beleiving that I shall receive full pardon & free remission of all my sins & be and by the pretious deth & merits of my blessed Saviour & Redeemer Christ Jesus & my body to the Earth for when it was taken to be buried in such decent & Christian manner as to my Executrx. hereafter named shall be thought meet & convenient; And as touching such worldly Estate as the Lord in his mercy hath lent me, my will & meaning is the same shall be employed & bestowed as hereafter by this my Will is expressed, my just Debts first paid

Imprs. I give & bequeath unto my Eldest Son, RICHARD CAUTHORNE, & his heirs forever the one halfe of five hundred acres of land wch: was acknowledged by Capt. THO: GOLDMAN being part of a dividend of Two and Twenty hundred acres lying upon the head of HODGINS POCOSON

It. I give & bequeath unto my Son, THOMAS CAUTHORNE, & his heires forever the other halfe of my above sd Land

It. I will & desire that the rest of my Estate be equally devided between my Children

It. I doe ordaine & appoint my deare & loveing Wife, ANN CAWTHORNE, to be the

Executrx. of this my last Will & Testamt. revokeing & annulling by these presents all &
every Testamt; or Testamts. Will or Wills heretofore by mee made or declared either by
Word or Writing and this is to be taken only for my last Will & Testamt. & none other In
Witness whereof I have hereunto sett my hand & affixed my seale this 18th day of
March 1679.80
Signed & sealed in the presence of us
          EDMUND CRASK   RICHARD CAUTHORNE
          ROBT. [?][?]GULLOCK
    Proved by Comparison of hands the 3 day March 1686/7 in Rappa County Court and
Record the 24th

p.   Virginia the 29th 1686/7
117   IN THE NAME OF GOD Amen I EDWARD JOHNSON of the County of Rappa. & Parish
        of Farnham being very sick of body but of health & memory praised be God for
it, do make this my last Will & Testamt: revokeing all other Wills in forme following.
  Imprs. I bequeath my Soule to Christ my Redeemer & my body to Christian buriall
according to the Discretion of my Executrs: hereafter menconed
  I leave unto WM. MACONICO three cowes & one heyfer & one yearling being upon the
Plantacon of ENNIS MACONICO & one mare bigg with foale & one bed & what belongeth
to it & all other things that doth belong to me the abovesd Cattle to be delivered in kind
when he cometh to the age of Sixteen. And the mare to run with encrease from the day
of the date hereof. And do make CHARLES DODSON my full Executr: to see this my Will
fulfilled when my Debts is satisfied & what is left to return to ENNIS MACANICO As Witness my hand & seale this 29th of Janry. 1686/7
Test DANLL: EVERARD   EDWARD JOHNSON
        ALEXAND: —— DUKE,
        PETER ⟵ ELMORE
  The above ALEXANDR: DUKE hath this day sworne that the sd EDWARD JOHNSON published this as his last Will & Testamt: & that he saw it sealed & delivered & although he
did not see him write his name yett he owned it as his name before me this 27th day of
Feb: 1686/7   SAMLL. TRAVERS
  Wee the Subscribers do depose & say that wee saw the within Testatr. signe seale &
publish the within Will & Testamt: as his last Will & that he was in prfect sence &
memory at the time of signing & sealing the same
                                PETER ⟵ ELMORE
                                DANLL. EVERARD
  Probatr p Sacramt. ELMORE et EVERARD in Cur Com Rappa 2 die Martii Ano Dom 1686/7
et Recordt. 18 die

p.   IN THE NAME OF GOD Amen. I ROBERT PARKER of the Parish of Sittenburne in
118   the County of Rappa., Plantr., do make & acknowledge this my last Will & Testa-
        mt. revoking all other Wills & Testamts. heretofore made
First I commend my Soule to God who gave it and my body to be decently buried at the
discretion of my Executrx. my worldly Estate I give & bequeath in manner & forme
following
  My Wife to enjoy the home Plantacon during her life but all my land being Eight
hundred acres by computacon, I give & bequeath unto my four Children to each of
them Two hundred acres still reserving to my Wife the Plantacon for her life, then to
my Son, JOHN, to have his first choise of Two hundred acres of land out of the said Eight
hundred acres which sd Two hundred acres I give unto him & his heires forever, so also

unto the other three Children save only if any of my three Daughters dye before marriage or the age of Twenty then their parts of land I give unto my Son & his heires forever, but if my sd Son shall dye beofre he be of age I give my land to be equally divided between my surviveing Children to them & their heires forever

My Cattle I give to be equally divided between my Wife & my sd foure Children. The Tobb: I have I give to buy a younge Negro; my goods household stuff Mill & the rest of my Estate I give unto my loveing Wife only a Negroe to each of them my Children after their Mothers decease;

Lastly I do make my Wife sole Executrx. of this my last Will & Testamt. wch: I confirme by my hand and seale this 15th day of Janry 1686/7.

Signed sealed & acknowledged in the presence of us

    ED: KEETING,

    (UNREADABLE)

    CALEB LYON his marke

                    ROBT. PARKER

                    his marke

SARAH LYON makes Oath upon the Holy Evangilists that she stood by & saw the within Testator sign seale & publish the within Will as his last Will & Testamt. and that he was of perfect sence & memory at the signing & sealing the same & further sayeth not

                    SARAH LYON

                    her marke

Probatr p Sacramt. LYON in Cur Com Rappa 2 die Martii Ano Dom 1686/7 et Record 14 die

        Test. WM. COLSTON, Cl Cur

ADAMS. John 47.
ADCOCK. Edward 72.
AINS. Thomas (Servant -35).
ALEXANDER. John 72.
ALLEN. John 60; Nathaniel 23, 34, 73, 77;
  Valentine 60.
ALMOND. John 73.
AMOSE. John 36.
ANDREWS. George 41; James 57.
ANSWATH. John 60.
APPLEBY. Richard 15, 71.
ARNOLD. Thomas 39.
ASCOUGH. Chrs. 78.
ASHTON. Elizabeth 1; James 1, 14;
  John (Will of -1); John (Capt. -1).
ATKINS. Alexander 71.
AUSTIN. Henry 16.
AWBREY. Henry 7, 13, 36, 45, 46, 57, 67,
  69, 73, 74.

BACKHAM. John 73.
BAICON. John 57.
BAKER. George 86.
BALLIN. John 86.
BARBER. Mr. 54; William 16, 23, 24, 54, 55,
  62, 80, 81, 82.
BARGIMAN. William 79.
BARNS. Timothy 15.
BARROW. Alexander 52, 53; Cicelly 52;
  Honer 52; John (Will of -52, 53);
  Jonathan 52; Mary 52; Moses 52.
BASSE 2; Michael 67.
BATES -73; John 7.
BATTAILE. John 73.
BATTIN. John 71, 76.
BAXTER. Book of 65.
BAYLEY (BAILY). John 16, 17, 24, 46, 48, 61,
  62, 65, 66, 71, 72, 76; Mr. 2; Robert 84;
  Robert Junr. 16; Samuel 46, 71, 79, 80, 81,
  84, 85.
BAYLIS. Catherine 85; John 62; Robert
  Junr. 71; Thomas 71, 85.
BEARBLOCK. John 2; Mr. 1, 2; William 2.
BEARE. John 62.
BEATSON. John (Servant-32).
BECKLEY. Joseph 70.
BEDFORD. Grace 16.
BENDRY (BANDRY). William 73.
BERRY. William 27.

BILLINGTON. Anthony 71; Barbara 84;
  Luke (Will of -84).
BLACK. James 28.
BLAGG. Abraham 66; Edward 66; Margrett 66.
BLAKE. John 85.
BLOMFIELD. Elizabeth 26; Mr. 60;
  Samuel 7, (Capt. -26); 45, 46, 57, 64, 73., 74,83.
BOLSTON. Thomas (Servant - 24).
BONKITT. John 38.
BONNER. John 28.
BOOTH. Thomas (Servant -31).
BORNE. Daniell 6.
BOULWARE. Ja: 76.
BOWEN. Alexander 74; John (Will of -74);
  John (Younger -74); Martha 74; Mathew 74;
  Stephen 74.
BOWER. John 4.
BOWLER. John 4; Tabitha 71.
BOWLES. John 71.
BOYCE. Dorothy 68, 69; George 36, (Will of -
  68), 69, 73.
BOYER. Andrew 32, 48.
BRASEY. William 83.
BRAT. Samuell 2.
BRAY. Richard 7, 38, 61.
BREAD. Thomas 71.
BRIDGETT. Land of 72.
BROCKENBURROUGH. William 48, 55, 71.
BROOKE. John 73; Robert 29, 30; Thomas 60.
BROWNE. Elizabeth 31; Frances (Moss -78);
  John 31, 49; Maxfield 30; William 31, 38,
  40, 41, 78.
BUMBREY. Thomas 1.
BURCH. John 15.
BURKETT. John 53, 57.
BURR. David 60.
BUSH. Abraham 21, 22.
BUTCHER. John 38.
BUTLER. John 76.
BUTTON. Thomas 13.

CALE. Mrs. 54.
CARDEN. Elizabeth 53; Robert (Will of -53);
  Robert (Younger -53)
CARNABY. Anthony 73.
CARTER. Edward 73; William 73.
CARTY. Denis 15, 16, 18, 24, 71; Mr. 60, 84.
CASH. Robert 83.
CASSANBOUGH. William 28.
CASTOR. William 47.

CATLETT. John 25, (Colnll. -39), 40, 61;
John (Younger -40), 41.
CAUTHURNE. Ann 86; Richard (Will of -86);
Richard (Younger -86); Thomas 86.
CHAPLE. Henry 61.
CHICHLEY. Sr. Henry 60.
CHISELL. Joseph 58.
CHITTY. Katherin 16; Thomas 16, 17, 62;
Thomas Junyor 16.
CHURCHES: Lower Scittenbourne Parish 69.
CLAPHAM. Mary 30; Mr. 35; William 30.
CLARK. Book by 71; Henry 54, 80;
Henry (Younger -80); Joane (Will of -5, 6);
John 4, 5, 6; Nicho: 52; Robert 54, 62.
COGHILL. David 63; Frederick 63;
James (Will of -63); James (Younger -63);
Margaret 63; Mary 63; Mary (Younger -63);
William 63.
COLELOUGH (COLCLOUGH). George 27, 34.
COLLEDGE. Hezechia 61; Hezekie 39.
COLLINS. John 77.
COLLY. Thomas 54, 62.
COLSTON. William (Cl Cur -15), 35, 61, 64, 83,
85, 88.
COMPTON. John 33.
CONDON. Ann 48.
CONWAY. Edwin 18, 71.
COOK. John 28.
COOPER. Capt. 70.
COPE. Michell 65.
CORBIN. Gawin 60.
CORNISH. Joseph 60.
COTHERN -60.
COUNTIES: Glocester 73; Lancaster 60;
Northumberland 49, 60; Westmoreland 61.
COVINGTON. William 69.
CRAIDON. Mr. 60.
CRASK. Capt. 60, 61; Edmund (Cl Cur Rappa:
-1), 2, 7, (Will of -12, 13), 20, 87;
Elizabeth 12, 13, (Will of -19, 20), 50, 59;
Ellen 12, 13, 20; John 12, 13, 20.
CREEKS: Farnham 47; Gilsons 27; Great 33;
Hodgkins 27; Rappa: 48; Totaskey 17, 80.
CROSSWELL. Gilbert 83; William 71.
CROW. John 84.
CUNSTABLE. Nicho: 17.
CUNSTOCK. Edmund (Alias Indian Ned -36).
CURTIS. Margarett 26, 27.

DACRES. Charles 71; Doctr: 52.

DALE. Ruben 62.
DANGERFIELD. Frances 68; John 57, 68, 73;
Mr. 73.
DAVIS. Edward 3, 73; Humphrey 53; Jos: 85;
Joshua 46; Richard 69; Robert 71.
DAWSON. William 12.
DAY. Mary 9.
DEALE. Reuben 34.
DEANE. Jane 5, 30; John 4, 5, 38; John
(Elder -4); John Junr. 5, 30; Mr. 29.
DERY. John 76.
DOBYNS. Daniel 69, 78.
DODING. Andrew 9.
DODSON. Charles 83, 87.
DONIPHAN. Alexander 5, 7, 16, 37, 74, 78.
DOWNING. Ralph 66, 71.
DOWNMAN. Peter 3.
DRAKE. Richard 62.
DRAPER. Josias 61.
DUDLEY. Alexander 16, 23, 54; Richard 54,
80, 81; Thomas 80, 81.
DUE (DEW). Andrew 47, 48, 62, 81;
Thomas 47, 62, 81.
DUKE. Alexander 87.
DUNBAR. Mr. 70.
DUNCOMBE. Jane 47.

EARLY. Denis 1.
EDGHILL. Robt. 61.
EDMONDSON. Thomas 43, 82.
EDRINGTON. Christopher 49, 67;
Margrit (Will of -49, 50).
EFFORD. Zacharia 81.
ELDER. Peter 54, 76.
ELLIS. Peter 54, 55, 71.
ELLIT. Richard 61.
ELMORE. Francis 61; Peter 87.
ENGLISH. Alexander 61; John (Blacksmith -2),
23.
ERWIN. John 61.
EVANS. Elizabeth (Peale -42); John 41, (Will
of -42); John (Younger -42); Rees 2, 5, 39, 85;
Rice 71; Saml. (Servant -24); William 42.
EVERARD. Daniell 87.

FANTLEROY. Katherine 79, 80;
William 62, 79, 80.
FENLEY. Thomas 63.
FENNELL. John 78.
FERGUSON. John 73.

FIELD. Abraham 4; Henry 4.
FITZ GARRALL. Gerrard (Servant -35), 72.
FITZHERBERT. William 72.
FITZHUGH. Colnll. 70; William 73.
FITZJEFFRIES. William 82.
FLEEPE. Rice 9.
FLEWELLING. Thomas 34.
FLOYD. Samuell (Will of -31, 32).
FORBES. Arthur 56, 73.
FOULKS. Mr. 73.
FOUNTAIN. James 79.
FOWLES. Capt. 61.
FOX. Capt. 60.
FOXHALL. John 30.
FOXON. Peter 52
FRACK. Martha 49; William (Will of -49).
FRANKS. George 73.
FRENCH. Nicho: 36; Richard 35.
FRISTOE. David 71.
FULLER. Susanna 81; Thomas 81.

GAINES. Bernard 39, 40; Daniell (Capt.) 25, 26, 34, (Will of 39, 40; Margret 39, 40; Margret (Elder) 40; Mary 39, 40; Robert 38.
GAMES. Daniell 5; Robert 7; Thomas 9.
GANFALLOW. Peter 56.
GANIONS. Thomas (Servant -30).
GANNOCK. William 3.
GARDNER. Elizabeth 66; John 67; Luke 67; Richard 67.
GARTON. John 37.
GATEWOOD. John 73.
GEORG -33; Edmond 70; Elizabeth 17, 23, 24; Leroy 17; Margaret 17; Mr. 62; Thomas 16, (Will of -17, 18), 23, 24.
GERRARD. Samll. 60, 61.
GESPER. Richard 55.
GIBSON. John 45; Magdallen (Will of -76), 77.
GILBERT. John 73.
GLASCOCK. Ann 51; Frances 51; Nicho: 51; Thomas 51, 71.
GLEN. William 55.
GLOVER. Mr. 2; Richard 71.
GODSON. Frances (Will of -72).
GOLDMAN. Mr. 61; Thomas (Capt. -86).
GOLDMARSH. Barbarra 26.
GOOD. Richard 37.
GOODRICH. Charles 1; John 73; Joseph 68, 73.
GOOGE (GOUGE). John 44, 69; Richard 73.
GORMAN. Henry 25.

GOSS -64.
GOWER. Ann 5, 6; Francis 6; Francis (Elder -6); Stanley 6.
GRACE -68.
GRAY. Abner 3; John 77; Simm 60; Will. 3.
GRAYDON. Joanna 86; Ralph 80, 81.
GREAT BRITAIN: Dublin 61; Ireland 48; London 1, 60, 65.
CREDIT. James 7.
GREEN. Ralph 73; Richard 12.
GREENSTED (GRINSTED). Richard 8, 9.
GRIFFIN. Janet 43; John 43; Leroy 21, 22, 24, (Coll. 71), 72, 79; Samuel (Colnll.-79); William 4, 43; William (Elder -4), (Will of -43)
GUBB. Micah 82; Nathaniel (Will of 82)
GULLOCK. Jane 29, 30; Robert (Will of 29, 30), 35, 36, 87.
GUNSTOCKER. Edward (Will of 75).

HACKENREE. Henry 62.
HACKER. Henry 62.
HALSEY. William 73.
HAMMEN. Thomas (Servant -38).
HAMMOND. Job 71; Martin 71; Susan 21, 33, 37.
HAMO. A Turk 45.
HANINGS. Phillip 18.
HANSFORD. John 81.
HARDING. William 73.
HARINGER. Joseph 82.
HARPER. John 28, 43; Mary 28; Saloman 28; Thomas (Will of -28), 42; Widdow 73.
HARRIS. Charles 75; Mr. 61.
HARRISON. James 21, 43, 45, 46, 62, 67, 73.
HART. Thomas 6
HARTLEY. Henry 83.
HARWAR. Thomas 35, 78.
HAWKINS. John 16, (Servant -24).
HEATHER. William 25, 42, 84.
HEFFORD. Zacharia 81.
HEINE. Book by 64.
HENINGS. Joseph 49; Robert 60.
HENLEY. Elizabeth (Will of -23); Robert 23, 54, 55.
HENSHAW. Samuell 25, 26.
HERBERT. John 71; Thomas 13, 19, 20, (Will of -30).
HEWETT. Thomas 85.
HICKS. Charles 75.
HILL. John 45.

HOBBS. Richard 10, 33.

HOBSON. Thomas (Cl Cur Northumberland Co. -
    49). 75.

HODGES. Arthur 82.

HOME. John 34.

HONSSING. Mr. 61.

HOOMES. David 23.

HOOP. Thomas 64.

HOPE. Mary 64; Thomas 64.

HORNBY. Daniel 71.

HUBBART. Doctr. 36; Moses 74.

HULL. Mary 75; Rebecca (Willoughby -75);
    Sarah 75.

HUMMINGS. Lawrence 84, 85.

HUTCHINGS. Richard 71.

INDIANS: Edward Gunstocker Will -75;
    Expedition against 75; Indian Ned 36.

INGOE. John 62.

INGRAM. Tho: 3; Tobias 1, 30, 77.

JACK. Patrick 34.

JACKSON. Daniell 32; James 21, 43; John 70.

JACOB. John 16, 17.

JACOBUS. Angell 5, 12; Elizabeth 5;
    Elizabeth (Elder -5), 6.

JANIWAY. John 64.

JASPER. Richard 71.

JEFFERSON. Joseph 81.

JEFFREY. Edward 71.

JENNINGS. John 49, 50, 67;
    William 49, 50, 67.

JESPER. Richard 16, 62.

JOHNSON. Charles 76; Edward (Will of 57);
    Martin 26, 34, 42, 83; Martin Junr. 73;
    Mary 26; Oswald 56; Peter (Will of -21), 33;
    Peter (Younger -21); Thomas 28, 42;
    William 60.

JONES. Cadwallader 3, 14; Colnll. 70;
    Edward 54, 55, 71, 85; Elizabeth 5, 85;
    Georg 3, 5, 10, 45, 46, 60, 66, 74; Honoria 3,
    46, (Will of -66, 67); John 8, 9, 73;
    Morgan 54; Robert 36, 37; Roddrick 16, 17,
    54, 71, 76; Samford 85; Thomas 31;
    William 50, 53, 55.

JORDAN. Hen: 69.

KEETING. Ed: 88.

KEISER (KEYSER). Mr. 60; Timothy 2.

KELLY. Mathew 47.

KENDALL. Thomas 84.

KEY (KAY). James 60, 75.

KING(E). James 19; Jane (Will of -30, 31), 57;
    John 8, 56; Richard 16, 71; Robert 18, 51.

KIRTON -60; Thomas 61.

KNIGHT. Elizabeth 23.

LAMPKINS. George 60.

LAND. James 9; John (Capt. -73).

LANKHORNE (LINKHORNE). John 21.

LASBY. Matt: 64.

LAWSON. Joshua 32; Josias 48.

LEE. Richard 79.

LEIGHTON. Richard 1.

LEWCAS. Henry 71.

LEWIS. Edward 16, 17, 71.

LIBB. John 73.

LINCOLN. Catherine 83; Elizabeth 83;
    Elizabeth (Younger -82); John (Will of -82), 83;
    John (Younger -83); Margaret 83.

LINDSEY. William 73.

LODOWICK. Walter 69.

LOFLIN. John 51.

LORD. Capt. 38.

LOYD(S). Colo. 11, 82; Lieut. Coll. 13;
    Marmaduke 73; Will: 2, 12, 13, (Col.-34), 39,
    47, 48, 61, 62, 71, 74.

LYON. Caleb 88; Sarah 88.

McCARTY. Denis 12.

McDONNOGH. Teige 84.

McKENNY. Carnough (Servant -8).

MACARTY. Dan: 76; Denis 16.

MACKARLE. George 73.

MACKENNY. Will: 8.

MACONICO. Ennis 82; William 82.

MAFFITT. John (Wheelright, Will of -44).

MAISEY. John 71.

MALLETT. Daniell 6.

MALLEY. Daniel 76.

MALPASS. John C. 73.

MAN. Christopher 63.

MARKES. Richard 73.

MARSHALL. Thomas 60.

MARTIN. John 21.

MARYLAND: Choptank 47.

MASON. John 44; Josiah 31; Mary 44;
    Thomas 76.

MASSESS. Robert 1

MASSEY. John 55, 71.

MATHEWS. Giles 38, 68; Richard 4, 7, 22; Thomas (Capt.-48); William 60.

MIDDLETON. Martin 23.

MILLER. Isabella 14; John 14; Margaret 14; Margaret (Elder-14); Susanna 14; Symon (Will mentd. -13), (Capt. -14); Symon (Younger) 13. William 14.

MILLS. Henry 7, 8; James 7, 8; Jane 8; John 5, 6, (Will of -7), 8; John (Younger -7), 51, 59, 83; Martha 8; Robert 7, 56, 73; William 34.

MINDLEN. John 73.

MOORE. Mr. 2, 70.

MORGAN. Elizabeth 30; Evan (Will of 30, 31), 38, 39.

MORRAH. John (Will of -16) 17).

MOSELEY. Edward 45; Mr. 3; William 62.

MOSS. Elizabeth 12, 19, 20, 38, 39, 73; Frances 12, 19, 20, 50, 58, 59, 73, 78; Rebecca 19; Robert 1, 20, 35, 36, 44, 45, 59; Thomas 19; William 19, 37, 45, 46, (Will of -58, 59), 78; William (Younger) 58, 59.

MOTLEY. John 7, 37, 38.

MOTLIN. Henry 22; John (Will of -22, 23); John (Younger -22); William 22.

MOTT. Mr. 43.

MUNCASTER. Henry 36.

MUNDAY. Thomas 36.

MURRALL. George 19.

MURROW. William 40, 41.

NASH. Henry 71.

NAYLOR. Thomas 60.

NESBUTT. Edward 75.

NEW. Thomas (Dept. Cl Cur -10), 12, 18, 19, 20, 51, 58, 59, 78.

NEWLON. Henry 13.

NEWMAN. Alexander 2, 60, 71, 79; John 2; Thomas 37, 58, 78.

NEWTON. Henry 20, 50; Elizabeth 20, 50.

NIGHTENGALL. Richard 73.

NOELL. Colo. 34.

NORINGTON. John 39.

NORTH. Anthony 7, 57, 73, 74.

NORTHERN. Edmund 6.

NORTON. Patrick 58.

OAKLEY. John 71.

OCKLY. John Senr. 51, 52; John Junr. 51.

ONBY. Andrew 67; Arthur 1, 38, 73.

ONELY. John 71.

ORCHARD. James 33, 38, 71.

OVERTON. John 71.

OWENS. John 62.

PACEY. Thomas 73.

PAGE. Jonas (Will of -80); Thomas 60.

PAGETT. John 73.

PALMER. John (Will of -80), 81.

PARK(E). Mrs. Joane 4, (Will of -5, 6); Robert 54.

PARKER. Jeremiah 68; Robert 19, 36, (Will of -87); Thomas 19, 20, 26, 28, 35, 36, 53, 68, 69, 74; Thomas Senr. 20, 73, 77.

PATE. Thoroughgood 48, 49.

PARTRIDGE. John 71.

PAVEY. Walter 54, 71.

PAVINER. John Junr. 83.

PAYNE. John 22; Robert 29; William 6, 38, 76.

PAYS. Robert 36.

PEACHEY. George 41; Mr. 76; Samuel 12, 15, 16, 34, 54, 55, 61, 65, 71, 72, 79, 80.

PEACOCK. John 15, 47, 73; Richard 16, 54, 55, 71, 76; Sarah 73.

PEALE. Elizabeth 42; Mallachy 30, 31, 71; William 42.

PEDLAR. George 60.

PEIRCE. Fran: 36.

PENDLETON. Phill: 73.

PERKINS. Thomas 5, (Will of 26), (Clerk -34).

PERRY. James 71.

PETERS. Parnall 43; Randolph 26, 27.

PETERSON. John 80.

PHILLIPS. Jeremiah 62.

PITMAN. William 49.

PLACES: Barbadoes 16; Cabin Point 52; Cherry Point 79; Exeter Lodge 60; Ferry from Town 60; Nomany 60; Forrest 4; Hodgins Pocoson 86; Matrums Neck 33; New England 16; Poplar Neck 45; Pumans Inn 14; Range Land 13, 68; Rappa: Ford 1; Sampsons Store 65; Stony Hill 47

PLAY (PLEY). George 13; Luke 71; Robert 13, 34, 35, 36, 45, 57, 76.

POND. Elizabeth 85.

POOLE. Mr. 3.

POPE. Humphrey 7.

POWELL. Book of 65; John 61, 62.

POWER(S). Francis 12; Margt. 39.
PRIDHAM. Ann 54; Christopher 54.
PRITCHARD. James 15.
PRITT (PRID). Robert (Will of ~48, 49).
PRITTLEE (PUTLEE). Mary 56;
  Nicholas (Will of ~56), 73.
PROSSER. Anthony 14; Mr. 14.
PURVIS. Georg (Capt. ~38), 71;
  John (Capt. ~71).

QUARLES. Fran: 66, 71; John 66, 71.
QUESTENBERRY. John 73.
QUIZENBORGH. John 7.

RABLLYS. Accomodation at 60.
RADFORD. Bowen 47.
RANE. Thomas 70.
READING. Robert 73.
REEVES. Henry 73.
REYLEY. Katherine 86.
REYNOLDS (RENNOLDS). Cornelius (Will of
  ~64), 69, 70; Doctor 14; John 60, 64;
  Margery 64, 70; Mrs. 56; William 64.
RICE. Ann 47, 48, 55, 62, (Will of ~81, 82);
  Dominick 1, 15, 16, (Will of ~47), 48, 55,
  62, 71, 81; John 35, 46, 60, 61, 65, 66, 71,
  72, 86; Mr. 60; Rebecca 85; Richard
  Junr. 48; Richard Senr. 48; Stephen 47, 48.
RICHARDS. Bridgett (Will of ~54); John 7, 71;
  Lewis 54; Mr. 7.
RICHARDSON. Elizabeth 22; Knight 23, 38;
  Roger 52.
RIDGE. Griffeth (Servant ~8).
RIVERS: Nomany 60; Rappa: 6.
ROBERTS. Elias 33; John 8; Mr. 60;
  Thomas 8.
ROBINS. Alexander 20, (Will of 27, 28);
  Alexander (Younger ~27), 28; Ann 20, 27;
  Elizabeth 27, 28; Judith 27; Judith
  (Wife ~28); Rebecca 27, 28.
ROBINSON. An 84; Elias 86; John (Servant
  ~30), 39; Max: 60; Mr. 82; Samuel 86;
  Susan (Servant ~24); William 15, 84.
ROLT(S). John 36, (Capt. ~47), 48, 62.
ROSE. John 30.
ROSS. Robert 1.
ROWLEY. Rowland 60.
ROWZEE. Edward 29, 30, 73; Elizabeth 29;
  Ralph 40, 73, 74.
RUDDERFORD. Robert 1, 73.

RUSSELL. Mr. 3.

SAMFORD. James 54, 71, 85.
SAMPSON. Isaack 64, 65; Jacob 64, 65;
  John 2, 61, (Will of ~64, 65); Ptolomious 65;
  Rebecca 64, 65; Store of 65, 71; Thomas 60.
SANDERS. John 22.
SANDFORD (SANFORD). James 54, 82.
SARGENT. William 39.
SAVAGE. Anthony 31, 39, 62, 70; John 60.
SAVIN. Acct. of 60; John 61.
SCOTT. James 6, 7; Robert 60; Walter 47.
SCURLOCK. Michael 31.
SEABRIGHT ~70.
SEARL. George 60; Thomas 21.
SEATES. James 6.
SERGENT (SARGENT) George 3, 4; William (Will
  of ~3), 4, 5, 6, 9, 10, 26.
SERVANTS 35, 43, 46; Thomas Ains 35;
  Bess a Negro woman 79; Black Bess, a Negro
  girl 45; Boy Servant 77; James Fountain 79;
  Gerrard Fitzgarrall 35; Thomas Ganions 30;
  Grace 68; Wm. Greenhill 79; Thomas Hammen
  38; Thomas Hewett 85; Hamo, a Turk 45;
  Man Servant 77; Carnough McKenny 8;
  Negroes two men 77; Old man 79; very old
  women 45, 79; Griffeth Ridge 8; John Robinson
  30; Secundus, a Negro man 45; Robert
  Vincent 49; Woman Servant 77, 79.
SETTLE. John 79.
SHERLOCK. John 71.
SHERRIT. William 2.
SHERWOOD. Mr. 60.
SHIPLEY. Alice 69; Daniel 6, 68, 69;
  Sarah 68.
SHIPS: Exeter Merchant 82; Loves Increase 81.
SHREWSBY. William 60.
SHURLOCK. John 60.
SISSEN. Mrs. 34; Robert 12; William 34.
SKELDERMAN. Harman (Will of ~37).
SLAUGHTER. Francis 23, 83; William 12, 15,
  65, 71, 72, 86.
SMITH (SMYTH). Ann 27; Anthony 8, 9, 27;
  Elizabeth 34, 72; Henry (Will of ~33),
  (Major 34, 35), 71; Henry (Younger ~33), 72;
  John 7, 39, 40, 41, 57; John (Elder) 40;
  Samuel (Lt. Colo. ~49); Toby 33, 72;
  William 47, 61.
SMOOT. John 71.
SNEAD. Charles 32.

SOAPER. John 71.
SOUTHEN. George 7, 46.
SPENCER. Colnll. 60, 61; Nicholas (Honrble. Colnll.-70)
SPICER. Arthur 18, 23, 47; John 22.
STALLARD. Samuell 41; Sarah 41; Winifred 41; Walter (Will of -41)
STEPP (STAPP). Abraham 20, 57; Martha 20.
STEPTOE. Anthony 2.
STERNE (STARNE). David 4, 7, 10, 22, 47, 57, 61; Frances 4, 10; Francis 7.
STEWARD. John 28, 73.
STOAKES. Ellinor 19; Rebecca 20; Richard 19, 20.
STONE. Elizabeth 50; Francis 38, 50, 61, 68; John 5, (Coll. -6), 10, 46, 64, 74; William 71.
STONHAM. Henry 68.
STRIPT -12.
STRONG. John 73.
STROTHER. William 39.
SUGGETT. John 12, 65, 66, 76; Mr. 71; Sarah 64.
SUTTLE. Fran: 48.
SWAMPS: Deep 7; Great 4; Nimcock Valley 7.
SWAN. Alexander 2, 12, 15, 16, 34, 61, 62, 65, 66; Mr. 82.
SWINBURN. Thomas 1.
SYNOCK. Doctr: 1, 7; Mr. 3.

TANDEY. Henry 28, 73; Mr., Junr. 73.
TARRANT. William 6, 73.
TAVERNER. John 18, 35, 61, 64, 66, 71, 72, 76.
TAYLOE. Will: 79.
TAYLOR. Francis 32, 33; George (Capt. -5), 6, 7, 19, 37, 38, 45, 46, 51, 58, 64, 67, 73, 78, 79, 80; Henry 82; James 14, 15; Martha 5; Richard 73; Thomas 71, (Will of -85); William (Under Sheriff, Colo. 48).
THOMAS. Christopher 38, 62; Edmd. 16; Edward 70; Job 12, 60
THOMPSON (TOMPSON). Francis 61; Thomas 71.
THORN. Rowland 34.
THORNBURY. Mr. 82; William 34.
THORNTON. Ducke 48; Francis 14, 15, 39; Jerimia 48, 49; Rowland 70, 73.
THRESHLEY. Thomas 73.
TILLEY. Henry 80.
TOMAZIN. Simon 70..

TOMLIN. Nathaniell 14; Robert Junr. 12, 71.
TOMPKINS (TOMKINS). James 34, 36, 38.
TOWNSEND. Joseph 60.
TRAVERS. Hezekiah 60; Mathew 60; Rawleigh 85, 86; Samuell 61, 76, 79, 80, 85, 86, 87; William (Collo. -60), 61, (Will of -85, 86).
TRENT -60; Alice 23; James 6, 7, 16, 22, 23.
TUNE. Ann 47, 81; James 47; John 47; Mark 47; William 81.
TURCKE. Nath: 71.
TURNER. Hezichia 61.

UNDERWOOD. Joane 53; William 25, 33; William Junr. 53; William Senr. 53.

VASSALL. John (Colo. -66).
VAULX. (Gullock) 29; Mary 30; Robert 30.
VICKERS. John 60.
VINCENT. Robert (Servant -49).

WALKER. Thomas 54.
WALLOW. Samuell 76.
WALTER. Robert 71.
WARD. Bryan 1, 42, 68; Margrett 42; William 6.
WARDON. Joseph 16; Thomas 16.
WARREN. John 4, 7; Will: 4.
WATERS. John 43, 50; John Junr. 50; Roger 16, 34, (Doctr., Will of 51, 52), 71.
WATKINS. Henry 28.
WATSON. Elizabeth 24, 25; John 1, (Will of -24, 25), 26; John (Younger -24), 25; Mr. 73; Priscilla 24, 25; Susan 24, 25; Thomas 24, 25.
WATTS. Richard 67.
WEARE. Nicholas 70.
WEBB. Giles 16, 71; Isaac 71, 85; John 34, 85; Robert 77, 78.
WEBBER. Mr. 55; Robert 51.
WEBLEY. Thomas 44.
WEIRE. John 5, (Majr: -46), 66; John (Younger -46).
WELCH. John 80.
WELLS. Barnaby 4, 7, 58, 78; Grace 78; John 73, 74; Rebeccah 4.
WEST. Richard 1, 42.
WESTBURY. Edward 59.
WETHER. Mr. 61.
WETHERBURNE. Edward 54.

WHEELER. Humphrey 82; Thomas 9;
  William 21, 60.
WHITE. Arabella 44, 77; Dorcas 44;
  Henry 1, (Will of -44); Ignatius 47;
  Majr. 60; Thomas 85.
WHITHEAD. Samuel 16, 62, 81.
WHITING. Ralph 39, 71.
WHITLOW. Ralph 69.
WHITRIDGE. John 4; William 4.
WILKS. Thomas 16.
WILLIAM(S). Fran: 74; John 7, 29;
  Susana 28; Thomas (Capt. -70)
WILLIAMSON. Henry 9, 78.
WILLOUGHBY. Henry (Doctr)(Will of -75);
  Rebecca 75.
WILSON. Charles 78; Elias 37, 59;
  Henry 16; Michaell 71.
WINTER. Richard 71.

WITHERS. John   (Will of 83, 84);
  Margarett 84; Sarah 84.
WITT. William 81.
WOFFENDALL. Adam 39.
WOOD. John 6; Richard 60; Thomas 68;
  William 60.
WOODBRIDG(E). Paul (Majr: 1), 2, 55, 62.
WORMLY. Christopher (Coll. -61); Ralph 60.
WORTH. John 60.
WRIGHT. Isaac 71; Maria 54.
WITHITER. Richard 71.

YATES (YEATS). James 35, (Will of -70);
  Nicholas 1.
YOUNGE. William 35, 60, 78.

Heritage Books by Ruth and Sam Sparacio:

Abstracts of Account Books of Edward Dixon, Merchant of Port Royal, Virginia, Volume I: 1743–1747

Abstracts of Account Books of Edward Dixon, Merchant of Port Royal, Virginia, Volume II

Albemarle County, Virginia Deed and Will Book Abstracts, 1748–1752

Albemarle County, Virginia Deed Book Abstracts, 1758–1761

Albemarle County, Virginia Deed Book Abstracts, 1761–1764

Albemarle County, Virginia Deed Book Abstracts, 1764–1768

Albemarle County, Virginia Deed Book Abstracts, 1768–1770

Albemarle County, Virginia Deed Book Abstracts, 1776–1778

Albemarle County, Virginia Deed Book Abstracts, 1778–1780

Albemarle County, Virginia Deed Book Abstracts, 1780–1783

Albemarle County, Virginia Deed Book Abstracts, 1787–1790

Albemarle County, Virginia Deed Book Abstracts, 1790–1791

Albemarle County, Virginia Deed Book Abstracts, 1791–1793

Augusta County, Virginia Land Tax Books, 1782–1788

Augusta County, Virginia Land Tax Books, 1788–1790

Amherst County, Virginia Land Tax Books, 1789–1791

Caroline County, Virginia Order Book Abstracts, 1765

Caroline County, Virginia Order Book Abstracts, 1767–1768

Caroline County, Virginia Order Book Abstracts, 1768–1770

Caroline County, Virginia Order Book Abstracts, 1770–1771

Caroline County, Virginia Order Book, 1765–1767

Caroline County, Virginia Order Book, 1771–1772

Caroline County, Virginia Order Book, 1786–1787

Caroline County, Virginia Order Book, 1787, Part 1

Caroline County, Virginia Order Book, 1788

Culpeper County, Virginia Deed Book Abstracts, 1795–1796

Culpeper County, Virginia Land Tax Book, 1782–1786

Culpeper County, Virginia Land Tax Book, 1787–1789

Culpeper County, Virginia Minute Book, 1763–1764

Digest of Family Relationships, 1650–1692, from Virginia County Court Records

Digest of Family Relationships, 1720–1750, from Virginia County Court Records

Digest of Family Relationships, 1750–1763, from Virginia County Court Records

Digest of Family Relationships, 1764–1775, from Virginia County Court Records

Essex County, Virginia Deed and Will Abstracts, 1695–1697

Essex County, Virginia Deed and Will Abstracts, 1697–1699

Essex County, Virginia Deed and Will Abstracts, 1699–1701

Essex County, Virginia Deed and Will Abstracts, 1701–1703

Essex County, Virginia Deed and Will Abstracts, 1745–1749

Essex County, Virginia Deed and Will Book, 1692–1693

Essex County, Virginia Deed and Will Book, 1693–1694

Essex County, Virginia Deed and Will Book, 1694–1695

Essex County, Virginia Deed and Will Book, 1753–1754 and 1750

Essex County, Virginia Deed Book, 1724–1728

Essex County, Virginia Deed Book, 1728–1733

Essex County, Virginia Deed Book, 1733–1738

Essex County, Virginia Deed Book, 1738–1742

Essex County, Virginia Deed Book, 1742–1745

Essex County, Virginia Deed Book, 1749–1751

Essex County, Virginia Deed Book, 1751–1753

Essex County, Virginia Land Trials Abstracts, 1711–1716 and 1715–1741

Essex County, Virginia Order Book Abstracts, 1699–1702

Essex County, Virginia Order Book Abstracts, 1716–1723, Part 1

Essex County, Virginia Order Book Abstracts, 1716–1723, Part 2

Essex County, Virginia Order Book Abstracts, 1716–1723, Part 3

Essex County, Virginia Order Book Abstracts, 1716–1723, Part 4

Essex County, Virginia Order Book Abstracts, 1723–1725, Part 1

Essex County, Virginia Order Book Abstracts, 1723–1725, Part 2

Essex County, Virginia Order Book Abstracts, 1725–1729, Part 1

Essex County, Virginia Order Book Abstracts, 1727–1729

Essex County, Virginia Order Book, 1695–1699

Fairfax County, Virginia Deed Abstracts, 1799–1800 and 1803–1804

Fairfax County, Virginia Deed Abstracts, 1804–1805

Fairfax County, Virginia Deed Book Abstracts, 1799

Fairfax County, Virginia Deed Book, 1798–1799

Fairfax County, Virginia Land Causes, 1788–1824

Fauquier County, Virginia Minute Book, 1759–1761

Fauquier County, Virginia Minute Book, 1761–1762

Fauquier County, Virginia Minute Book, 1766–1767

Fauquier County, Virginia Minute Book, 1767–1769

Fauquier County, Virginia Minute Book, 1769–1771

Hanover County, Virginia Land Tax Book, 1782–1788

Hanover County, Virginia Land Tax Book, 1789–1793

Hanover County, Virginia Land Tax Book, 1793–1796

King George County, Virginia Order Book Abstracts, 1721–1723

King George County, Virginia Deed Book Abstracts, 1721–1735

King George County, Virginia Deed Book Abstracts, 1735–1752

King George County, Virginia Deed Book Abstracts, 1753–1773

King George County, Virginia Will Book Abstracts, 1752–1780

King William County, Virginia Record Book, 1702–1705

King William County, Virginia Record Book, 1705–1721

King William County, Virginia Record Book, 1722 and 1785–1786

Lancaster County, Virginia Deed and Will Book, 1652–1657

Lancaster County, Virginia Deed and Will Book, 1654–1661

Lancaster County, Virginia Deed and Will Book, 1661–1702 (1661–1666 and 1699–1702)

Lancaster County, Virginia Deed Book Abstracts, 1701–1706

Lancaster County, Virginia Deed Book, 1710–1714

Lancaster County, Virginia Order Book Abstracts, 1656–1661

Lancaster County, Virginia Order Book Abstracts, 1662–1666

Lancaster County, Virginia Order Book Abstracts, 1666–1669

Lancaster County, Virginia Order Book Abstracts, 1670–1674

Lancaster County, Virginia Order Book Abstracts, 1674–1678

Lancaster County, Virginia Order Book Abstracts, 1678–1681

Lancaster County, Virginia Order Book Abstracts, 1682–1687

Lancaster County, Virginia Order Book Abstracts, 1729–1732

Lancaster County, Virginia Order Book Abstracts, 1736–1739

Lancaster County, Virginia Order Book Abstracts, 1739–1742

Lancaster County, Virginia Order Book, 1687–1691

Lancaster County, Virginia Order Book, 1691–1695

Lancaster County, Virginia Order Book, 1695–1699

Lancaster County, Virginia Order Book, 1699–1701

Lancaster County, Virginia Order Book, 1701–1703

Lancaster County, Virginia Order Book, 1703–1706

Lancaster County, Virginia Order Book, 1732–1736

Lancaster County, Virginia Will Book, 1675–1689

Loudoun County, Virginia Order Book, 1763–1764

Loudoun County, Virginia Order Book, 1764

Louisa County, Virginia Deed Book, 1744–1746

Louisa County, Virginia Order Book, 1742–1744

Madison County, Virginia Deed Book Abstracts, 1793–1804

Madison County, Virginia Deed Book, 1793–1813, and Marriage Bonds, 1793–1800

Middlesex County, Virginia Deed Book, 1679–1688

Middlesex County, Virginia Deed Book, 1688–1694

Middlesex County, Virginia Deed Book, 1694–1703

Middlesex County, Virginia Deed Book, 1703–1709

Middlesex County, Virginia Deed Book, 1709–1720

Middlesex County, Virginia Order Book, 1686–1690

Middlesex County, Virginia Record Book, 1721–1813

Northumberland County, Virginia Deed and Will Book, 1650–1655

Northumberland County, Virginia Deed and Will Book, 1655–1658

Northumberland County, Virginia Deed and Will Book, 1662–1666

Northumberland County, Virginia Deed and Will Book, 1666–1670

Northumberland County, Virginia Deed and Will Book, 1670–1672 and 1706–1711

Northumberland County, Virginia Deed and Will Book, 1711–1712

Northumberland County, Virginia Order Book, 1652–1657

Northumberland County, Virginia Order Book, 1657–1661

Northumberland County, Virginia Order Book, 1665–1669

Northumberland County, Virginia Order Book, 1669–1673

Northumberland County, Virginia Order Book, 1680–1683

Northumberland County, Virginia Order Book, 1683–1686

Northumberland County, Virginia Order Book, 1699–1700

Northumberland County, Virginia Order Book, 1700–1702

Northumberland County, Virginia Order Book, 1702–1704

Orange County, Virginia Deeds, 1743–1759

Orange County, Virginia Order Book Abstracts 1747–1748

Orange County, Virginia Order Book Abstracts 1752–1753

Prince William County, Virginia Deed Book, 1749–1752

Prince William County, Virginia Order Book Abstracts, 1752–1753

Prince William County, Virginia Order Book Abstracts, 1753–1757

(Old) Rappahannock County, Virginia Deed and Will Book Abstracts, 1656–1662

(Old) Rappahannock County, Virginia Deed and Will Book Abstracts, 1662–1665

(Old) Rappahannock County, Virginia Deed and Will Book Abstracts, 1663–1668

(Old) Rappahannock County, Virginia Deed and Will Book Abstracts, 1665–1677

(Old) Rappahannock County, Virginia Deed and Will Book Abstracts, 1668–1670

(Old) Rappahannock County, Virginia Deed and Will Book Abstracts, 1670–1672

(Old) Rappahannock County, Virginia Deed and Will Book Abstracts, 1672–1673/4

(Old) Rappahannock County, Virginia Deed and Will Book Abstracts, 1673/4–1676

(Old) Rappahannock County, Virginia Deed and Will Book Abstracts, 1677–1678/9

(Old) Rappahannock County, Virginia Deed and Will Book Abstracts, 1678/9–1682

(Old) Rappahannock County, Virginia Deed and Will Book Abstracts, 1682–1686

(Old) Rappahannock County, Virginia Deed and Will Book Abstracts, 1686–1688

(Old) Rappahannock County, Virginia Deed and Will Book Abstracts, 1688–1692

(Old) Rappahannock County, Virginia Order Book Abstracts, 1683–1685

(Old) Rappahannock County, Virginia Order Book, 1689–1692

(Old) Rappahannock County, Virginia Will Book, 1682–1687

Richmond County, Virginia Deed Book Abstracts, 1692–1695

Richmond County, Virginia Deed Book Abstracts, 1695–1701

Richmond County, Virginia Deed Book Abstracts, 1701–1704

Richmond County, Virginia Deed Book Abstracts, 1705–1708

Richmond County, Virginia Deed Book Abstracts, 1708–1711

Richmond County, Virginia Deed Book Abstracts, 1711–1714

Richmond County, Virginia Deed Book Abstracts, 1715–1718

Richmond County, Virginia Deed Book Abstracts, 1718–1719

Richmond County, Virginia Deed Book Abstracts, 1719–1721

Richmond County, Virginia Deed Book Abstracts, 1721–1725

Richmond County, Virginia Order Book Abstracts, 1694–1697

Richmond County, Virginia Order Book Abstracts, 1697–1699

Richmond County, Virginia Order Book abstracts, 1699–1701

Richmond County, Virginia Order Book Abstracts, 1714–1715

Richmond County, Virginia Order Book Abstracts, 1719–1721

Richmond County, Virginia Order Book, 1692–1694

Richmond County, Virginia Order Book, 1702–1704

Richmond County, Virginia Order Book, 1717–1718

Richmond County, Virginia Order Book, 1718–1719

Spotsylvania County, Virginia Deed Book, 1722–1725

Spotsylvania County, Virginia Deed Book, 1725–1728

Spotsylvania County, Virginia Deed Book: 1730–1731

Spotsylvania County, Virginia Order Book Abstracts, 1742–1744

Spotsylvania County, Virginia Order Book Abstracts, 1744–1746

Stafford County, Virginia Deed and Will Book, 1686–1689

Stafford County, Virginia Deed and Will Book, 1689–1693

Stafford County, Virginia Deed and Will Book, 1699–1709

Stafford County, Virginia Deed and Will Book, 1780–1786, and Scheme Book Orders, 1790–1793

Stafford County, Virginia Deed Book, 1722–1728 and 1755–1765

Stafford County, Virginia Order Book, 1664–1668 and 1689–1690

Stafford County, Virginia Order Book, 1691–1692

Stafford County, Virginia Order Book, 1692–1693

Stafford County, Virginia Will Book, 1729–1748

Stafford County, Virginia Will Book, 1748–1767

Westmoreland County, Virginia Deed and Will Abstracts, 1723–1726

Westmoreland County, Virginia Deed and Will Abstracts, 1726–1729

Westmoreland County, Virginia Deed and Will Abstracts, 1729–1732

Westmoreland County, Virginia Deed and Will Abstracts, 1732–1734

Westmoreland County, Virginia Deed and Will Abstracts, 1734–1736

Westmoreland County, Virginia Deed and Will Abstracts, 1736–1740

Westmoreland County, Virginia Deed and Will Abstracts, 1740–1742

Westmoreland County, Virginia Deed and Will Abstracts, 1742–1745

Westmoreland County, Virginia Deed and Will Abstracts, 1745–1747

Westmoreland County, Virginia Deed and Will Abstracts, 1747–1748

Westmoreland County, Virginia Deed and Will Abstracts, 1749–1751

Westmoreland County, Virginia Deed and Will Abstracts, 1751–1754

Westmoreland County, Virginia Deed and Will Abstracts, 1754–1756

Westmoreland County, Virginia Order Book, 1705–1707

Westmoreland County, Virginia Order Book, 1707–1709

Westmoreland County, Virginia Order Book, 1709–1712

www.ingramcontent.com/pod-product-compliance
Lightning Source LLC
Chambersburg PA
CBHW081158270326
41930CB00014B/3210